Choosing You~~r Words~~
Crafting Yo~~ur~~

A compilation of affirmations and stories designed to nurture and empower.

Jean A Costa

The profits from the sale of this book supports the Duke Cancer Patient Support Program's Pink Ribbon Yoga Retreat. The annual retreat, founded in 2005, was formed to bring together women fighting breast cancer—from those who are newly diagnosed to women who have been thriving for decades. Through a shared yoga journey women from all over the country find support, camaraderie, healing joy and peace. To remove financial barriers that could prevent participation, this four-day retreat is offered at a low cost and provides scholarships for those who need additional support.

Affirmation Press

ISBN: 978-1-944662-55-4

Previous ISBN: 978-1-4575-5218-2

Printed in the United States of America

In Jean Costa's latest book, *Choosing Your Words, Crafting Your Life*, she reminds the reader of two valuable but perhaps forgotten inner resources for self-nourishment: the abilities to choose and to craft. When we choose positive, energizing words and images, we craft a positive, energizing life.

This not only affects us but all those around us, which makes us, literally, instruments of peace and reconciliation. The "how" of this process is clearly visible in Jean's sharing of her own lived experience. This book provides an inspiring example of someone who makes a daily practice of choosing her words and, as a result, has crafted a life that nourishes many others.

Sister Mary Margaret Weber, CSC
Co-Founder and Co-Director of A Place for Women to Gather, a not-for-profit ministry sponsored by the Sisters of the Holy Cross.

This book could be used as a "Life Guide" for anyone seeking balance in their life. It could also be used as a "Coaching Guide" for professional business coaches working to provide support to those around them. This book is a must-read, which I would highly recommend to anyone seeking a higher purpose in life.

Done E. Vance, COO Hound Ears Club

Whether I am teaching Sunday School, speaking to an audience representing countries from around the globe, or taking advantage of a teachable moment with my son, the subject matter has a common thread—stories. Stories passed down through the ages with nuggets that can be life-changing if we are open to them. Stories that help us to become better leaders and better people. Stories we are building each day by the choices we make.

Jean Costa's stories and affirmations in *Choosing Your Words, Crafting Your Life* are a powerful and personal example of the importance of choice in our lives. It helped me to read each affirmation and story and then take some time to reflect on each one. Thank you, Jean, for sharing your gifts and stories with the world. We are all better off from it!

Oie Osterkamp
Executive Director
Ronald McDonald House of Durham, NC

God created everything by speaking. God created us to be like Him. Jean shares how she has created her successful life and how journaling has enabled her to direct her thoughts to create the life she desires. Each of us can create what we believe in and focus on our internal dialogue and conversations with others. This book creates a positive foundation for you to focus your thoughts and words to create your best life!

Lea Strickland, MBA MA CMA CFM CBM, Author, Speaker, Entrepreneur, and Talk Show Host, President/CEO F.O.C.U.S. Resources, Cary, NC

Contents

Dedication

To my husband, Sandy,
and our children,
Melissa, Joey, and Ellen.

Foreword

Thank you to Jean Costa for another remarkable blessing bestowed upon us all with her newest book: *Choosing Your Words, Crafting Your Life*. Journaling through each season, Jean wryly observes life's obstacles and gifts with her special blend of humor, honesty, and compassion. Beyond the smile-inducing insights and moving anecdotes, Jean offers powerful affirmations we all can apply to transform our thinking and empower our lives.

A growing body of research documents that "self-talk" plays a fundamental role in how you perceive yourself and the world around you. In your mental monologues, you may often disparage and demotivate yourself. Have you caught yourself uttering these words? "How could I be so stupid!" "I'm a loser." "This always happens to me." This interior chatter is widespread in our society. When we habitually use this language, we paint ourselves as victims and fools, enfeebled and hopeless. The more we disparage ourselves, the more we embed this negative persona. We believe what we say! If you could record and play out loud this negative chatter in your head, you might be shocked by your words and tone. You would never tolerate this verbal abuse if someone else were haranguing you! Yet how ironic that you would choose to verbally abuse yourself.

This negative "self-talk" not only diminishes how we perceive ourselves internally, it actually affects us externally. Studies show this negativity undermines our happiness, diminishes our performance at work and play, deflects us from our goals, and frays our ties with family and friends. It corrodes how we see the world around us—judgmental, harsh, unfair, and unforgiving. We inhabit the negative and embrace our shrunken "shadow" selves.

But as Jean demonstrates so vividly, we have a choice. We can flip the switch in our brain. Instead of beating ourselves down, Jean shows how we can lift ourselves up. Jean demonstrates how all of us can shift our mental monologue to a positive one. The world is unchanged—still filled with tragedy, joy, monotony, confusion, and clarity. But the way we perceive the world changes. The way we perceive our place in the world changes. We learn how to affirm our BEST selves, achieve our goals, and strengthen our bonds with family and friends. It starts with the words we choose and leads to the life we craft.

With charm and wit, Jean shares her hard-won lessons in a way that is vulnerable and accessible. She translates these lessons into language we can adapt to create new mental monologues. With her guidance, you can shed words of self-disparagement and switch to words of compassion, wonder, and joy. By choosing this new approach, you can embrace the abundance of the world and your positive role in it. Over time, using Jean's approach, you will develop habits to be happier, kinder, and bolder in spirit.

I have read the book twice, and will keep it on my bedside so I can benefit from her nurturing again and again. With Jean's book, awareness unfolds and faith deepens. We each can choose how to define ourselves, and create a life of "peace and exhilaration." I know, I will be sending this gift to my family and dearest friends.

Ellan Cates-Smith
Media & presentation coach to leaders of Fortune 500 companies
Delray Beach, Florida and Cambridge, Massachusetts

WELCOME

The May/June 2015 issue of *Where to Retire* had an article about practices recommended to help one develop habits to improve the quality of one's life. One of the suggestions was to create affirmations. The example they used revolved around the discipline of daily exercise. Now, everyone knows that a body needs to move in order to stay healthy. There are some who say exercise is the fountain of youth, and others say that if there was a way to bottle all the benefits of exercise and turn them into pill form, it would be like an elixir of the gods. Knowing and doing, however, are two very different things. What guidance could the article offer to get people more involved in exercise? I was pleased to see their approach was to reframe what you said to yourself about an activity. According to the article, if you tell yourself you're a swimmer, runner, walker, tennis player, golfer, etc., you will be more likely to pursue that activity. Not only will you be telling yourself what type of athlete you are, you'll probably use those same words to describe yourself to others. It's about the process of labeling ourselves, and don't we all do that with or without intention and most times not to our benefit?

Choosing Our Words, Crafting Our Lives reflects my wholehearted belief that what we choose to say to ourselves and about ourselves affects every aspect of our being, all the way to our cellular structure. When we choose those words and phrases that nurture and empower us, our whole being responds to them.

While preparing for the Barnes and Noble signing of my first book, *Creating Positive Affirmations, Living an Intentional Life*, I asked myself, "What makes you think you're someone who can inspire or motivate another to live an intentional life?"

Truth to tell, I am simply another human being, probably a lot like you, who is trying to live a rich, joyful, compassionate life. My mission statement for my life is "I live a Christ-centered life of love, peace, joy, hope, gratitude, and compassion." And every day I have to remind myself of it and of how I want to live. It's a meditation. It's something I have to keep in mind every day, sometimes every moment. Do I? Of course I don't.

I know I'm not an expert on human behavior. I have studied it for many years and I've worked with a lot of people in many different capacities. My degrees in education and social work are the foundation for what I like to study. One of my first loves is a study group. I facilitated my first study group at Barnes and Noble in Cary, North Carolina, in 1997. The group studied the book *The Artist's Way* by Julia Cameron. We had around thirty-five people participate in the twelve-week session. Since then I've either facilitated or participated in hundreds of groups. From my observation I would propose that most people are trying to find a way to live a more fulfilled life. What that takes is, of course, different for different people, so I don't claim that I can offer everyone that opportunity. But there are some basic skills available to most of us, and using our words to shape our thoughts and, therefore, our lives is a very powerful one.

We are all talking to ourselves and each other all the time; sometimes it's an inner dialogue and other times it's out loud. With just a little effort we can start carefully choosing the worlds we use. You know what I'm saying. In fact, it's probably easier to shape the words we use to describe events and others than it is to shape those we use for ourselves. We can be our own worst enemies. I have a long list that I've collected of negative self-talk phrases, things I've heard people say to themselves or perhaps read somewhere. For example: "I am so stupid! I am such a klutz! I never seem to get it right. I just can't make any friends. I never have enough money, time, energy, etc. My right leg, arm, hip, etc. is my *bad* one." The list I've compiled has about one hundred negative phrases. Two others that don't sound negative but have that effect are, "I am right!" and "I can do that better." Those two statements may be true, but I'm here to tell you (and I know I'm right!) most people don't want to be around someone who has all the answers and who will willingly tell them how to do something better, even if they've been asked.

So, I'm not here to give you any answers. I am here to propose questions and to tell you what has worked for me. I want to share the practice and the words that have made my life better, not perfect, but definitely better. The positive affirmations I have created for myself and that I write about here and in my other book, *Creating Positive Affirmations, Living an Intentional Life*, have improved the quality of my relationships, my health, my work, and, perhaps most importantly, my faith. They aren't necessarily designed to improve your life. They simply serve as an example of what has worked for me and, in case you're searching, what may work for you.

I'm not speaking here of becoming narcissistic. I don't believe we are here to live lives of conceit and contempt. I believe we are here to be powerful through humility and service. One way to achieve that balance is to carefully choose our language. Louise Hay has been guiding us to powerful words and phrases for decades. Norman Vincent Peale wrote about positive thinking back in the 1970s. It's no different from exercise. It's a simple concept but it can be hard to put it into practice. Once you do, once you start to see the amazing, uplifting impact it has on your life, you won't want to live any other way.

I began writing about this practice because I felt I had discovered "the best shoe store in the world." These shoes were very good-looking, you could wear them forever, they never hurt, and they were on sale! That's how I felt about discovering positive affirmations. My life shifted. My mood shifted. My health and my relationships became better. I felt I had an obligation to share this tool with others. I know not everyone is interested in what I have to say, but I'm so excited about how this skill has made me feel, I need to shout about it.

Words! What words do you choose to label yourself with? I can as easily go down into those places of despair, sadness, and self-pity as the next person, but I have discovered that I can also recognize what I'm doing, thinking, and saying—and with some effort and practice, I can turn those phrases around and choose to create not just sentences that sound cheery and upbeat but a life that is rich and meaningful and marvelous. And who among us would not want to share those tools with others? Who does not want to help the world to a better place? Who doesn't want a cheap pair of the nicest, most comfortable "shoes" ever?

How to Create an Affirmation

If you have read my first book, *Creating Positive Affirmations, Living an Intentional Life,* you will have already read most of this information. If you are like me, however, you'll probably need a little reminding of how this process works.

One of the first steps to creating an affirmation is to take a look at your "self-talk." Notice those things you say to yourself throughout your day. Sometimes you're having the conversation when you're alone; sometimes you're not. What are the phrases you've adopted over the years? Are they empowering or demeaning? This book is about changing the negative things you tell yourself. You can do it! Anyone can do it. Why would you want to start saying positive things to yourself or about yourself? Will it make any difference? Yes, it will.

What exactly is an affirmation? What does it look like? How should it sound? What phrases work? Which ones do not? An affirmation is a statement that affirms (and makes firm) that which you believe. You can have positive or negative affirmations. Most of us have lived our lives telling ourselves about our faults. We also rarely hesitate to tell others about our faults.

Avoid Negatives

When creating an affirmation, avoid the word "not." It won't work to your benefit, and it may even work to your detriment. There are some phrases you can use instead of enlisting the negative. For example, "I release or I let go of." Two of my affirmations using those phrases are "I let go of fear and anxiety," and "I release myself from my childhood limitations." It's simply more effective than saying, "I will not let fear and anxiety influence my life." Can you hear the difference? Can you feel the difference? What are some things in your life you'd like to let go of or release?

I heard a story many years ago about a mother teaching her daughter to drive. There was a huge boulder in the road ahead. The mother kept reminding her daughter about it. "Don't go near the boulder," and "Don't hit the boulder." What do you think happened? They were both so focused on missing the rock in the road that they drove right into it.

The same thing can happen if you include negatives in your affirmation. You won't hear the "not" and you'll move right into the place you're trying to avoid.

Sometimes it's helpful to write out an affirmation without too much thought and then take time to fine-tune it. Begin by taking a few minutes and re-reading the words. You are looking for words that stir an emotion in you. Don't overanalyze. Let the sentence be a statement of how you want to perceive your life. It is very important to *write it in the present tense.* It may be a statement you have a difficult time believing, but try it anyway. Sometimes those affirmations are the most powerful. I have a dear friend whose affirmation is "I am a gifted and talented artist." When she first claimed it, she did not feel that way—but that's how she wanted to feel. It worked! She faked it until she made it. She now feels like the gifted and talented artist she is. Her affirmation led her to the steps that led her to believe in herself and to expand her gifts and talents.

Emotions

It is helpful to use words that resonate deeply within you. Try out some of the words; see if they cause a visceral reaction. One of my affirmations is related to the concept of staying connected to the Divine. I believe that we are spirit having a human experience and that with awareness and quiet we can connect to God's Divine Grace. You can define that any way you like. I believe it's available to us and can lead us to a peace beyond that of human comprehension. So I created the affirmation: "When I pray and meditate, I enter into union with the Divine; miracles are created and without struggle manifest themselves." I love the words *divine, miracles, without struggle,* and *manifest.* When I hear them I think *hope.* I have found that I now spend more time in prayer, more time in silence. Miracles? Oh, yes, they have manifested. Is it because I am paying more attention, waiting for them to appear, or is it because they have multiplied because of my time spent with Spirit? Do I really care why? Would you?

Then write them down! Put them in your journal. Put them on your computer. Put them on sticky notes and place them where you won't miss them; by your mirror, by the doorway, in the car. There is power in putting our words, intentions, and dreams on paper. You don't journal? Try it, and you might just discover a wonderful tool to enhance every aspect of your life. My practice is to write three pages every morning, longhand (cursive). I had to decide years ago how big or small those pages would be and how large or tiny my writing would be, but once I settled on a style, I discovered the joy of daily journaling. You don't need to journal to create your affirmations, but it's a very powerful place to let them gestate and to be born.

Don't think that the affirmations you create today will become tomorrow's reality. They need to percolate. First, they reside in your consciousness, then in your subconscious, and finally they settle into your cellular structure. Then, one day you have something happen that in the past may have depleted or upset you in some way, and instead, you come away feeling completely different. That's when you'll know the power of choosing your words to craft your life.

How This Book Is Organized

Choosing Your Words, Crafting Your Life is divided into the four seasons. There is one affirmation for each week of the year. These are some of my personal affirmations. Each one is followed by a story.

The intentions I share here are only to serve as an example. They may or may not resonate with you. Your life's focus may be very different from mine. Feel free to use any that do work for you.

As you can well imagine, there is a huge amount of information available on the Internet about affirmations. Once you begin the journey, inspiration will come from places you never even imagined. I believe God wants us to live full, rich lives. He/She does not want us to just drift along. We were created with minds and free wills so we could choose those things that best serve God and our brothers and sisters. By taking charge of our thoughts and therefore our behaviors, we are honoring God and bringing a richness to our lives and to all those whose lives we touch. This transformation would not occur if we did not make the effort to live an intentional life.

SPRING

1. Living an Intentional Life

Affirmation: *Every day I get to choose how I want to perceive my life experience.*

When Mo Martin won the 2014 Women's British Open at Royal Birkdale in England and was interviewed, she mentioned her "intention" was to win the tournament. At the time she was ranked 99th on the tour and it appeared no one had her listed as a potential champion. She ended her win and her final hole with an eagle, which means she had three shots on a hole on which a good golfer would normally have had five shots.

At the time of this writing, I was lucky enough to be in the mountains of North Carolina and once again I found myself playing golf. I have to work very hard in order to play golf somewhat decently, and in the past I've only worked on it for the few weeks I'm up in the mountains. I do, however, love the sport. I've usually shared the time with my husband, Sandy, and many times my son, Joey, comes with us. Sometimes his beautiful wife, Belen, also comes along. It's beautiful in the North Carolina mountains, and the course we've played on looks like a postcard. It's exhilarating when I actually hit that little ball and it soars away down the fairway toward the pin. I love it when I putt the ball and it rolls along and plops in the hole. I actually love to watch someone else make a long, difficult putt. It almost seems surreal to me to finally have that tiny ball fall into that tiny spot on this huge expanse of lawn. I think a big part of the excitement for me is that I'm so surprised and delighted when things actually go better than I even imagined.

I don't intend to have a low expectation of my performance, but after years of playing I have come to recognize that I will probably remain a below average player unless I decide to play more than just one month of the year. However, I always set an intention to do well and to enjoy the day.

The first time I heard the phrase "take an intention" it was at a yoga class many years ago. The teacher did not provide any other guidance; she simply told us to "take an intention for your practice" and then left us to figure it out. I remember it clearly. The word "gratitude" popped into my mind and so I embraced it and let it sit with me for the hour. Interestingly it didn't leave me at the end. I found it was with me as I went into the day, and here I sit many years later still embracing gratitude, every day.

When I teach I always follow that same example. I encourage everyone to chant an "ohm" and to bring their palms together in front of their heart. With their thumbs touching their heart, I say, "Take an intention for this time you're giving yourself. Any word that comes to mind is fine." And then at the end of our practice, we repeat the chant and I remind the participants to recall the intention they took at the beginning of class and encourage them to take it with them into their day, and perhaps into their lives.

That simple instruction so many years ago has had a very powerful impact on my life. I found myself taking an intention each morning for the day. As I journal and pray in the morning, I wait to see what word or words come to my awareness and I let them sit with me as I finish my quiet time and then bring them with me into my day. It's very seldom that something doesn't come to the surface. If not, I just let go for the day. I decided also that I might as well take an intention for each year. After quite a bit of reflection, each January I choose a phrase to take with me into the year. It has been a very interesting and rewarding practice. I write more about this in the Winter chapter, *Setting an Intention*.

When I listened to Mo Martin's interview, I found her expression of intent to be of interest. I assume she's a yogini. Maybe yes, maybe no, but yogini or not, she had a remarkable attitude. She "took an intention" to win! Yeah, Mo! Go, girl! Why not? She set herself up for success. She knew it was possible she wouldn't win, but once she set that intention, she recognized that she could very well achieve her goal. She also said even when she wasn't playing well, when she wasn't winning, she still woke up every day with a smile and a sense of excitement about being able to play.

Living an intentional life means you've given thought to what you want your life to look like. I would imagine if you're reading this, you already are someone who is choosing how to live your life, but don't assume that's how most of the world lives. Unfortunately, many people are faced with such dire challenges, they don't have the energy to focus on choice. Others simply have chosen not to choose but to let life and fate play themselves out. Once you begin taking an intention, you may find your day and, therefore, your life take on a richness that makes you feel like a winner no matter what challenge life presents. Or, at the very least, you wake up each morning, like Mo, with a smile on your face and a sense of excitement about being able to play the game of life.

2. A Place for Mystery

Affirmation: *I let mystery have a place in me.*

Terry Gross of NPR's Fresh Air was interviewing Bart Ehrman, a professor of religious studies at UNC, Chapel Hill. He had just written, *How Jesus Became God.* I had a feeling I knew where this interview was going, but I love to learn about anything to do with religion, any religion, and I love talk radio, so I stayed tuned in.

NPR had this introduction on their website: *When Bart Ehrman was a young Evangelical Christian, he wanted to know how God became a man, but now, as an agnostic and historian of early Christianity, he wants to know how a man became God.*

When and why did Jesus' followers start saying "Jesus as God" and what did they mean by that? His new book is called How Jesus Became God: The Exaltation of a Jewish Preacher from Galilee.

"In this book I actually do not take a stand on either the question of whether Jesus was God, or whether he was actually raised from the dead," Ehrman tells Fresh Air's Terry Gross. *"I leave open both questions because those are theological questions based on religious beliefs and I'm writing the book as a historian."*

I once gave up doubt for Lent. For me, it's easy to doubt. It seems to me that our egos are so involved in our identity that most of us believe we need to be able to understand everything. If we can't understand it, it must not be true. Over the years, however, I've discovered I actually understand very little. There is so much that is simply unknown. I could list all the questions I have about life and the Universe, but I'm sure you have many of your own. The simple question about what happens to us after we die is one very prominent unknown. It's one of life's greatest mysteries. I was surprised by my reaction to Professor Ehrman's interview. I know I have only that segment on which to base my response to his theories, but his words left me feeling very sad.

I did listen carefully. Certainly his research was factual. There didn't seem to be much one could dispute. He had gathered his facts carefully. His research confirmed his beliefs. Like the website stated, he had gone from being an Evangelical Christian to an atheist. It appears the New Testament gospel stories about what immediately took place after Jesus died are fictitious. Oh yes, Jesus was tortured, humiliated, and crucified, but there was no way he was then taken down from the cross after his death, placed in a tomb, and rose three days later. According to Roman tradition, that's just not how things were done back then. Back then? As far as I know that's not how things are done now. Rising from the dead sure isn't the norm even in today's world.

Father Alapati of Saint Michael's Catholic Church in Cary, NC, told this joke as part of his homily.

It appears a gentleman rose one morning to find his obituary in the paper. He was shocked and immediately called his friend and said, "Did you see my obituary in today's paper?" His friend responded, "Yes, but where are you calling from, heaven or hell?"

Facts supporting the Resurrection would be lovely. The Apostle Thomas seemed to feel the same way. "But he said unto them, Except I shall see in his hands the print of the nails, and put my finger into the print of the nails, and thrust my hand into his side, I will not believe" (John 20:25). I've always been fascinated by the Apostles. So afraid, so timid, so uneducated, hiding away in a room somewhere, waiting for those angry crowds to come and pull them off to the same torture and death their leader just endured. I can feel the fear. I can almost taste it. We've seen what angry crowds do. It's in all parts of the world. I would be terrified. What happened to change them so? What facts can be gathered to explain why they would leave that room and go out into the crowds and begin to preach the Good News? These men (and let's hope a woman or two) left their safe space and changed the world forever. How does one explain that? It's a mystery.

My fellow yoga teacher, friend, and mentor, Nancy Hannah, shared with me a saying with which her mother, Bunny Stone, would guide her. "Let mystery have its place in you." According to Nancy, her mom was a remarkable woman who made amazing inroads and created life-changing programs here in North Carolina. In Rachel Remen's *The Will to Live and Other Mysteries* she writes about the fact that our western culture is more a culture of mastery than mystery, but life is more about mystery than mastery. Most of us, however, refuse to recognize the mystery that permeates our lives. We need to understand all things, because by understanding we believe we are in control. It's a fallacy. After controlling our thought process, there is very little else of which we are in control.

How do our egos interfere in the really important values of our lives: peace, hope, love, gratitude, compassion, and, yes, faith? What facts are available to prove these qualities exist? Can we ask to place our hands into them, our fingers? Here is where faith must triumph over facts. Faith—trust on steroids—is believing in something completely irrational because one has let go of their ego. The test here is to decide to believe and to let God work within and through us. This is when we are called upon to let mystery have its place in us. I find comfort in my faith. I find peace. I like resting in the mystery and not trying to figure it all out. We might not be able to hold the proof in our hands, but if we choose, we can hold it in our hearts.

3. Hopes and Prayers

Affirmation: *I let go of resentment.*

Wayne Dyer, in his *Ten Secrets of Happiness,* tells his readers that one of the secrets is to affirm, "There are no justified resentments." That means we are called on to forgive every action that has bothered us, intentionally or unintentionally. How are you at doing that? Have you ever thought you were "over" something and then it reared its angry head when you least expected it? For me, I can nurse an injury to death! It can be years after the perceived hurt has occurred, and the name of the offender will cause me to sit up straight and grimace and relive, perhaps even re-tell, the horrible act committed. Boy! That will show that person. I will be justified and they will suffer because of my anger and my indignation. The truth is, however, there is only one person suffering—me—and I have created it myself.

I was discussing with a friend that several of her dear friends had not reached out to her and her husband after he had undergone surgery. She was angry. I understood. When I was treated for breast cancer, some of the people with whom I was closest never sent a note or picked up the phone. Hundreds (and I am not exaggerating) of people reached out with such caring and generosity. It was healing and affirming, but every now and then, I'd wonder about those few people who hadn't taken the time to even send me an email. When I thought of them, I'd feel resentment. I wondered why I chose to focus on those who appeared to ignore me and not the amazing people who showed such love and care?

This missive is being written in the season of Lent, 2015. I love Lent. I've felt this way for many years. It's a time of quiet. It's a time for additional reflection, a time to really focus on what is important to me in my relationship with God and others. It's a time for me to develop a new good habit or two. It's a time of hope. It is the dormant time before the rise of the flowers and the blossoming of the trees. It's that time when I wait with joyful anticipation for spring and the resurrection of Christ. It's a time when my heart feels full with what is to come.

Lent has taken on a very different meaning for me over the years. As a child we would be encouraged to give up some favorite food and also to fill a small paper box with coins for the hungry children of a far-off country. I'm sure I tried to honor the requests. I'm sure I didn't do too well at it either. Then, as a young adult I rebelled. I decided all those rules and regulations were silly. What purpose did it serve to give up anything and how much of a difference did my small contribution make to the poor and destitute of the world? The thing that helped me recognize the wisdom of my church's traditions was staying connected to my church. This is my home and one of the many gifts has been learning to honor our Lenten tradition.

I had taken two intentions for this Lent. The first was to dedicate each day to one person. Their name went on the top of my journal page and I wrote a small prayer for the person. If it seemed appropriate, I sent it to them. I told them that on this "nth" day of Lent I was lifting them up in prayer for the entire day. I told them how they blessed my life and how much I treasured their friendship and I ended with wishes for a day filled with love, peace, and joy and, many times, improved health. I sit, first thing in the morning, to see who comes to mind and I make that my person for the day. One day someone "appeared" with whom I had had quite a bit of struggle. I didn't want to offer up my day for that person. I didn't want to think about that person at all, much less keep her in my thoughts for an entire day. I felt myself retreat from the idea and question for whom else I might pray. Certainly, many other people deserved prayer more than that person.

The February 24th reading in *Spiritual Insights for Daily Living*, edited by Elizabeth Fenske, has a quote from the Mayo Clinic: "Three-fourths of our patients are passing on the sickness of their minds and their souls to their bodies." The reading goes on to say, "Be careful of the beliefs you hold and the thoughts you repeatedly think. In Proverbs (6:27) the writer asks, 'Can a man take fire unto his bosom, and his clothes not be burned?' More specifically, we can ask: can a man (or anyone) take fears, doubts, hatred, resentments, and worries into his mind, and his body be unaffected?

The Buddhist saying is, "When the student is ready, the teacher will appear." The teacher appeared in my reading and Jesus told us, "Forgive." How many times? "Seventy times seven" (Matthew 18:21).

At a recent Pink Ribbon Yoga[1] Committee planning meeting, Nancy Hannah, one of our dedicated, gifted yoga teachers, had us take the pain and suffering of others, surround it with love, and then breathe it transformed back out into the universe. I had been struggling with the suffering of our world. The 2015 news of twenty-one Coptic Christians being beheaded, people being put in cages and burned to death, and the stories of the girls and women being kidnaped and abused left me feeling weary and sad and powerless. What could I do to help the world?

USA Today on February 23rd of the same year had a marvelous story about a woman, Nareen Shammo, who gave up her job as a reporter and tirelessly worked toward the freedom, the salvation of any woman being held hostage. She was succeeding one woman at a time. I didn't feel I had that kind of power, but perhaps here on this page as I share my concerns, I can encourage and enlist those people who have chosen to read this book and *Creating Positive Affirmations, Living an Intentional Life* to join me in praying for them, praying for an end to war and hatred and religious intolerance. Use a rote prayer, make up a prayer, breathe prayerful energy into this world, but do something!

The second intention I adopted for Lent was: ***I let go of resentment.*** It meant I had to dig deep within and forgive those I have struggled with. It meant I must pray for not only those I comfortably hold in my heart but for those I don't want to embrace. It means I have to pray for my enemies and even the terrorists. Perhaps, through the power of prayer, a heart will soften, maybe many hearts and the torture and abuse of the innocents of our world will decrease. It all begins with me. It all begins with you.

So, I wrote down the name of the person that day for whom I didn't want to pray and I offered up the day for her well-being and that of her family because I "must be the change I wish to see in the world" (Mahatma Gandhi).

---

[1] A four-day retreat for women breast cancer survivors held every August at the North Carolina Beach, sponsored by Duke Hospital.

4. Seeking a Better Life

Affirmation: *I read something inspirational every night and motivational every morning.*

For four nights during the week before Holy Week, Father Jim Sichko from Texas spoke to over a thousand people in my church of St. Michael the Archangel in Cary, NC. We have a very large parish, over 16,000 people. The church has daily mass, Saturday evening mass, and five masses every Sunday. Our services are blessed with the gift of an amazing music minister, Wayne Cushner, and a dedicated group of choir members. I love going to mass. I've gone my whole life and I love the ritual. I find it comforting. I am also grateful for the gift of the Eucharist. I've seen my church's faults and I've chosen to stay and work at change from the inside out. I'm blessed to feel this way. I know not everyone can understand. I am one of the lucky ones. I was born into this faith in which I feel so at home.

Mass is an obligation for Catholics. We are told that if we miss mass without a legitimate reason, we have sinned. Father Sichko began his introduction to the parishioners by telling them they were welcome to leave if they were at the mass because of obligation and not because they wanted to attend. I'm not sure if he had the church's blessing on that direction, but I understood what he was saying: Don't show up without an attitude of gratitude. Embrace the gift. Embrace the mystery.

How many times have we shown up physically to some event but didn't commit emotionally? What we invest in our experience is directly proportional to what we receive from it. How about school for an example to which we can all relate? Everyone knows that the amount of time and effort one puts into one's education directly affects what one learns. Yes, it is easier for some than for others, but that isn't the point. If we aren't fully invested in the process, we miss out regardless of whether or not the learning comes easily. We may not only miss out on how much and what we learn from the classes but from our teachers, peers, and the environment.

Catholic mass is not an entertainment form. Regardless of the music or the priest's personality, it is a very traditional ritual. We stand, sit, and kneel, over and over. I've heard it called "Catholic aerobics." The readings change and the hymns are different weekly, but the words are always the same. I can go to mass anywhere in the world, and I have, and regardless of the language, I know most of what the priest is saying. I tell you this because I understand how other, more contemporary, fun services can attract people. I can understand why some people come to mass out of obligation and not out of want, and it is obvious when a church is filled with people who would like to be somewhere else. Many don't sing; they vie for seats in the back of the church; they don't bother to say the prayers; and they leave as soon as communion is distributed. I understand why Father Sichko gave permission to those unapprecia- tive Catholics to leave.

The people attending the mission were there because they wanted to be. How could I tell? People came early. A half hour before the mis- sion began, the church was almost full. Everyone sang—they were still singing after Father Sichko walked out of the service. It was an awesome sound. I stopped singing for a short time just to listen. It was like the Mormon Tabernacle Choir! All those people singing a joyful sound. Why, I wondered, did so many people choose to spend four evenings here in this church? What was of such value that they made an effort to attend? Certainly, this is not the first event of its type.

I've never attended a traveling preacher's event. Even living here in the heart of the Bible Belt, I've never gone to hear Billy Graham speak or Joel Osteen, who has regularly visited our area. My only revival expe- rience is from watching the movie *Elmer Gantry* with Charlton Heston a "hundred" years ago. I would hope that's not a good representation. From the little I remember he was not a very upright person. I can understand, however, how one can get caught up in the experience. I guess it is like the Super Bowl of faith. It's exciting, all these people gath- ered in one place with a similar outlook, rooting for the same team. But why are they here? What is everyone looking for? What do they hope to gain? People seem to be seeking something most of us cannot seem to find alone.

My mother was a great fan of Robert Schuller and the Crystal Cathedral. Thousands of people attended his services and millions watched every Sunday. Joel Osteen's church is a former basketball stadium and holds over 18,000 people. It is full every week and millions more have watched his services from home. You don't have to look to the media, however, for popular preachers or venues. Here in Cary alone we have other churches that attract large throngs of people each week. It's the same throughout the rest of the country. They represent every denomination: Protestant, Mormon, Jewish, Nondenominational, Muslim, etc. Why? Why are people coming together? Is it simply for community or are they looking for something else? Why do they return week after week, year after year? Why did over a thousand people come to St. Michael the Archangel every night for four nights the week before Holy Week? Was it because it was free? Maybe they had nothing better to do? No, I believe it was because we are all looking for something beyond ourselves, beyond our understanding, beyond our wildest imagination. We are looking for that which will complete us. I believe we are looking for God.

People came hoping. They were hoping they would hear something that would inspire them to lead richer, fuller lives. They wanted to know more about their faith with the hope that it would lead them to lives of more value. They wanted to know what knowledge their faith has gathered over the last two thousand years that would bless them and their loved ones today and in the future. Did they get that? Did they enrich their lives and their faith?

Father Sichko had a direct message, a simple one but not an easy one. He told us to "live the gospel." Have you read the gospels? Have you read the words of Jesus Christ? His lessons are very clear: care for the poor, the sick, the imprisoned, the suffering of this world. Love at all costs, all the time. Don't be attached to your material possessions and trust that God is always here to care for you. Simple, but challenging mandates. Father Sichko repeated these directives. He was able to weave them around some very entertaining stories, some very humbling stories, and at the end of the fourth night, he received a standing ovation. His message seemed to reach everyone there. It was an inspirational experience. The energy in the church was palpable. It was exciting! I knew I was in a holy place with others who chose to be there.

For the four nights of Father's presentation I was inspired. It was the difference between looking at a photo of a bowl of my favorite ice cream and actually being able to eat it. I had come looking for a way to enrich my life and to add to the blessings of my family and friends and perhaps some part of the world, and I found it. I found it in Father's reminder to "go live the gospel." I know I'll need reminding. I can only hope that some unappreciative Catholics did show up on a night or two and they, too, were inspired—to the point where they found themselves wanting to come to mass, not just because they thought they needed to in order to escape the everlasting fires of hell, but because something magical happened, something mystical. The veil that had hidden the blessings of their faith was pulled back, and they could finally see the beauty, the gift of the mass and especially of the Eucharist.

5. Being Worthy

Affirmation: *I am worthy.*

What determines the worthiness of a human being? In 1997 the movie *Gattaca* came out, starring Ethan Hawke. It was a sci-fi film about genetically altering the human fetus toward a specific occupation. A child who was born without this alteration was considered imperfect or inferior and was deigned useful only for menial jobs. Ethan was one of those children born without the advantage of the sophisticated science of the time. He was not happy with his predetermined role, and the movie revolves around what he needed to do to give the illusion of being one of the perfect people. As we all know, the science fiction of today often becomes the reality of tomorrow. With genetic testing widely available and with the mapping of the genome, the theme of *Gattaca* may not be too far removed from the very near future.

When I've facilitated programs about creating affirmations, people are encouraged to create phrases that do not have any negatives in them. A few years back, however, there was one person who had had a very difficult childhood and she decided she was going to use "not" in her affirmation because it was the best phrase to help her feel better, and so she did. It worked for her, but most of the time when we use a negative in an affirmation, our brains ignore the negative and we wind up doing or feeling exactly the opposite of what we had intended. She decided she did NOT need to do anything more or be anyone other than who she was to be of value. When she shared her affirmation it was obvious to everyone present that it was going to have a powerful impact for her, even with the word "not" as part of it.

When someone is asked, "What do you do?" the answer generally generates a visceral response in both the questioned and the questioner. Have you watched the physical response of both parties as this question is presented? Have you observed yourself? I've seen the persons being asked sometimes puff up, stand taller, perhaps their shoulders go back. I've watched some people slump over, maybe step back as if they're preparing for battle. Then there's the questioner's response to the answer. For example, if the answer is "I'm a brain surgeon" most people would probably have a different response than if the answer was "I'm a trash collector." We generally judge and many times value an individual based on what they *do*.

I am fascinated by society's value determination of occupations. As far as I'm concerned if people were financially rewarded for their services based on how they benefit society, sports persons would not be making millions of dollars while teachers eke out a living. Movie stars would not be some of the richest people in our country while those who care for the sick and elderly barely make minimum wage.

Where am I going with this? I want everyone to be feel valued simply because they are a human being. My friend was right. We don't need to do anything more or be anybody special to be worthy. We need to value each person simply because they are a creation of God. If we don't do that it would mean that the sick, the infirm, the elderly, the mentally ill are of no value. It will mean that someday society will allow science to genetically alter or design a human being, and those who don't come out "perfect" will be relegated to a subservient place or, even worse, destroyed.

My faith, the Catholic Church, promotes the sanctity of life from the womb to the tomb. I know this is not a popular concept and I understand how people because of dire circumstances sometimes want to be in charge of who lives and who dies and when, but it seems to me it's a slippery slope toward devaluing the human being and life itself.

Several years ago I was invited by a dear friend, Ann Baucom, to join her and a group of women in developing a personal "charter of compassion." I came up with six steps: pray, embrace silence, listen for God's voice, affirm what is important to me, release it into God's care, and love non-judgmentally, non-graspingly, and unconditionally. When I shared this charter with a friend, she thought it was too self-centered and not enough other-centered. But I feel I can't effect any change in the world until I change myself.

Each human being is a masterpiece, no matter what the flaws. The flaws can add color, depth, and texture. We are each a precious treasure and with that concept we should know that we are worthy—worthy of respect, worthy of love, worthy of all the good and prosperity of a

Divine creation. Once we believe in ourselves, we will possess the wherewithal to give back to the world.

We can be of service by simply knowing God is always with us and She is leading us and guiding us. If we are listening we will do it with love and honor and compassion. We are of service if daily we rise with the intention to bless the world in our thoughts and words and deeds. We can impact the world regardless of what we do or are unable to do if we simply hold our fellow man or woman in our thoughts with blessings and love. I am a perfect being created by a loving God regardless of what I do or don't do, and so are you!

6. Savoring Life

Affirmation: *I eat mindfully.*

Mindfulness is the practice of being fully aware of the present moment without judging. Jon Kabat-Zinn brought a greater awareness to the practice back in the 1970s when he began teaching mindfulness-based stress reduction (MBSR), which is still taught worldwide. I studied MBSR at Duke Integrative Medicine, NC, in 2000. It's a gift we give ourselves when we develop the ability to be in the present moment. It's also the practice of a lifetime. Most of us here in the West don't sit in a lotus position for several hours a day chanting or focusing on a mantra (a single word or phrase). Most Americans are more concerned about the past or the future and are missing whatever is happening in the present. In general, we are a busy, preoccupied population. Most of us, however, are also looking for ways to improve the quality of our lives. We are searching for that which will enhance our daily experiences and not leave us feeling so worn out and tired. We are looking for the tools we can use to fix or shape or color our lives so that we are able to take deeper breaths, appreciate the beauty of nature, and relish the precious moments of connection with those we love.

For many, prayer is a powerful tool. It's my first choice. Time to communicate with my God, time to tell Her my concerns, time to offer up thanksgiving for all my blessings, and time to simply sit and listen. It doesn't have to be formal prayer. My day is lifted up and given over to God, Jesus Christ, before I even rise from the bed. Then, if it's a day of unending activity, which I must confess is not unusual, I still know that I am in prayer mode throughout all the business.

In yoga the practitioner is called upon to focus on his or her breath. Sometimes a yoga practice may only involve pranayama, breathing techniques. There are many, some more elaborate than others. The simplest one involves watching one's breath. I encourage my students at the very beginning of practice to simply notice their breath. "Close your eyes and begin to focus on your breath, the in and the out, the up and the down, the rise and the fall." After years of beginning practice this way, I simply need to think the words and I feel calmer. When a group of us are all focusing on our breath at the same time, the energy level in the room changes from charged to serene.

Another breathing technique that can be used anywhere, anytime is to simply take a deep breath. Breathe all the way down into your belly and then release it. Want to make it even more effective? Sigh it out. Oh, not just a little sigh; make it a full "Haaaaa!" Don't believe it'll make a difference? Try it right now, do it a few times, and then just notice. Don't judge, just observe if you feel any different. I attach the name of Jesus to my deep breaths. It's a mini-prayer that I can do anywhere, anytime.

Journaling is also an opportunity for me to practice mindfulness. I like to have a large mug of tea next to me, my favorite spiral-bound journal, an easy flowing ballpoint pen, and a pleasant space. I usually write in my sun room. I have a nice chair and ottoman, and the room faces my garden, the bird feeders, and a small waterfall. It's a yellow room with much of my favorite memorabilia on the shelves. I begin with a prayer, the prayer at the end of this book, and then write my three pages. I am fully there in the time and space. It centers me for the day. It leaves me feeling grounded and calm.

Another way for me to practice mindfulness is when I am eating. It's a reciprocal process in that when I focus on the process of eating, my eating becomes healthier. I'm always fine-tuning my diet. I'm a moderate person, meaning I don't usually go overboard when I'm making changes. I'm a sure and steady kind of gal. I share this with you because while I know a lot about vegan diets and vegetarian diets, I have not fully embraced any restrictive form of eating. I avoid certain foods that I think aren't my best choices, like things with sugar, artificial colors, or flavorings, foods that are heavily salted or have preservatives. I try to eat mostly fresh vegetables, fruits, whole grains, fish and chicken. I love a glass of wine periodically, and sharing an ice cream with friends, or especially with a grandchild, is a real treat for me. I know how important it is to eat a "good" diet. I know it's also important to nourish the soul. I love dark chocolate. I'm also aware of the global impact my choices have on the rest of the world.

When I trained at Kripalu Center for Yoga and Health, breakfast was always silent. It was a very informative experience for me. I am a social eater. I love to sit with family and friends and share a meal and conversation. If there's no one around, I don't really care if I eat or not. I'm an "eat-to-live" person, not a "live-to-eat" person. In order to make the best food choices for me, I decided to simply pay close attention to the eating experience. Have you ever tried the raisin experiment? You place a single raisin in your mouth and you don't chew it. You allow it to dissolve very, very slowly. You notice the texture, the sweetness. You think about how it came to become a raisin, where it was grown, who harvested it. It can take ten or even fifteen minutes to eat that one raisin. It can bring you to a whole new appreciation for every bite you take.

What is your eating environment like? Do you take your time and savor each bite, or have you just gone through the drive-thru and are eating as you go? What's dinner like? Is the TV on or is the computer in front of you? What if you simply sat at the table and focused on the food you were putting into your mouth and your body? If you ate mindfully would your choices be different? Mine are. We are what we eat. What and how we feed our bodies, our minds, and our spirits determines every cell of our being. Slow down, breathe deeply, eat mindfully, and savor your life.

7. Is God a Feminist?

Affirmation: *I believe the world is a better place when the gifts of women are recognized and honored.*

During the second week of March 2013, the Catholic Church elected a new pope. Cardinal Jorge Mario Bergoglio became Pope Francis. It didn't seem to matter if you were a Catholic or not; the event dominated the headlines around the world. World headlines are normally dominated by some dreadful disaster or horrible tragedy. I found this focus on the election of a new pope to be more uplifting and inspirational. The election only took two days and five votes before white smoke, the symbol announcing a new pope, rose above the Sistine Chapel. Tens of thousands were there waiting in the rain for the news. Curiosity was abundant. There had been much speculation about who the new pope would be and now, we were to finally find out. The questions were about whether or not he would be a Vatican insider. Would he be from Europe as were most of the former popes or would he be from another continent? Would he be younger than popes of the past? Would he possess a conservative or a more liberal theological perspective? The questions and speculation were endless and went on for weeks. There was only one question no one was asking. Would the new pope be a man?

This same week of March there were at least two specials, one on *60 Minutes* and one on *Good Morning America*, about a new book that had just been released by the COO of Facebook, Sheryl Sandberg, *Lean In: Women, Work and the Will to Lead*. When asked if she was trying to reignite the feminist movement, she said, "Yes," citing the statistic that only 4 percent of the Fortune 500 companies were led by women and that women still only made seventy cents to the dollar that men make. "The woman's movement has stalled," she said.

This year of 2013 was also the 50th anniversary of Betty Friedan's book, *The Feminine Mystique*, which many attribute to the beginning of the women's movement.

Whether or not you consider yourself a feminist, you cannot deny that the role of women here in the United States and in many civilized parts of the world has changed. Many would argue it has not been for the better. Many would argue women have only begun to make inroads into being the dynamic, influential presence they need to be in order to bring more balance and compassion into our universe. It seems to be a topic with many emotional ties and not a simple one. Women's roles in the Catholic Church have always been a topic of discussion and controversy. Change comes very slowly to my church, but with the election of Pope Francis, I had renewed hope.

At the time of this entry, Francis had been pope only a short time. The one word that was repeated most often was "humility." His first act after being elected was to ask the throngs waiting in the rain to see him and to hear him was to ask for their prayers. Stories abound about his association with the poor, not just in name but in deed. He cares deeply about his people, us, the church. His theology is conservative. There will not be any changes made to the church's stand on the sacredness of life from the womb to the tomb. I can guarantee that. Perhaps, however, with his humility he will be more encompassing of the role of women in our church and see them as not just holding a place of service but also deserving a place of leadership. I once heard someone say that Jesus Christ was one of the earliest feminists. He promoted the ethical treatment of all people without regard to their status, race, or sex.

When my grandson Owen was thirteen, he asked his mom, Melissa, if I was a feminist. The word "feminist" was said with a tone of derision. "Why?" she asked. He told her it had been explained to him that feminists hate men. Thank heavens for the wisdom of my daughter. "Yes," she answered, "Grandma is a feminist. I am a feminist. Your stepfather and your grandfather are feminists." She went on to explain that a feminist doesn't hate men. A feminist promotes the well-being of all people regardless of their gender.

I received the message at an early age that I needed to be responsible for myself. I needed to be independent. It was before the feminist movement, but it was clear to me that I needed to find a way to care for myself. A married life, if I married, of total domesticity would tie me to the success or failure of another and of that relationship. Many women have suffered devastating losses because they did not take any steps to create a life whereby they could care not only for themselves but perhaps for others who might come to depend on them.

I clearly remember reading *The Feminine Mystique.* It was a time before the Internet, before Oprah Winfrey and Doctor Phil. I had just had a baby and quit my teaching job (not in that order) when we moved to Norwich, New York, a town of seven thousand people. I knew no one and I was lonely. I was lonely and I couldn't figure out why I was struggling. I had, I believed, everything I needed. The baby was healthy. I was healthy. My husband was kind and generous, and we were beginning a whole new life. Help! I think if I had already read Ms. Friedan's book, I would have wondered if my sense of frustration was created because of it but I had not. When I read it, I knew she had written some of it just for me. I was not alone. It gave me some comfort and a sense of hope.

I read that most men today want their wives to work. They want them to bring in another income. The days of *Leave It to Beaver, Dick Van Dyke* or even the more recent *Raymond* are gone. The main issue, however, is that women are still the main caregivers for the children and the home. It's a heavy load and I don't have any easy answers for how to lighten the burden other than to choose a partner who will willingly do their share. I am in awe of any single parent who manages not only to balance all their responsibilities but guides their children to successful, productive lives.

I know there are young women out there who never think about the opportunities they now have as being hard won by women and men before them, but they were hard won. If it weren't for their efforts, we wouldn't have women physicians, scientists, politicians, and attorneys. It needs to be remembered there are women in third-world countries who are very aware of the opportunities available to women in other parts of the world, and they can only dream about them.

Sheryl Sandberg's book and Betty Friedan's book lead women to believe they can have it all. I hope that's true. I hope it's true too that with the installation of Pope Francis, my church will finally recognize what it has been missing all these centuries. They haven't uplifted at least half of their population, the women of their church—so many of whom are keeping the faith alive and vibrant. Yes, I am a feminist. I'd like to see women priests. I'd like to see a woman pope. I'd like to see women being treated with respect and dignity and having the same opportunities as anyone else. Who knows, if my wishes are granted, maybe I'll even get to one day see a woman become president of the United States.

8. Mirrored Reflections

Affirmation: *I choose to see myself as beautiful.*

What is your reaction when you look in the mirror? Do you look? I know some people who avoid mirrors at all costs, and I know others who can't seem to turn away when they see their image. What if I told you that you can make a conscious decision about how you perceive your image?

When I wrote this entry it was the season of spring. North Carolina looks like the Garden of Eden or a fairyland during this time. Everything is in bloom. The dogwoods are breathtaking. The flowering pear, cherry, and apple trees are awesome. The azaleas, pink, white, and rose-colored, have just gone into full bloom, and all the bulbs, daffodils, crocuses, and tulips, to name a few, are up and showing off. Along with all this beauty comes the natural instinct of the birds and the bees. We had a flock of robins living in our wooded area, and one of them went insane. She, we believed, was protecting her nest by slamming her beak and her body into any of our windows that she perceived harbored an enemy. It went on for weeks. All day long, *thwack, thwack, thwack.* There wasn't a solution other than to wait it out; I know, I researched it and tried half a dozen suggestions. None of them worked. Her bird brain defense toward her reflection made me wonder how often my perception is so skewed that I, too, see what isn't the truth.

Did you hear about the Dove beauty patch? It was an ad on YouTube. Normally I skip the ads but this one caught my attention right away. I was intrigued. It showed a psychiatrist interviewing several young women and applying the Dove beauty patch to their upper arms and explaining to them how to use it over the next week or so. They were told the patch would make them feel more beautiful. The ladies videoed their reactions. The first few days they reported no significant changes, but by the end of the trial period, they all reported an increased sense of well-being. They felt more beautiful. The psychiatrist then showed them the secret ingredient in the patch. Can you guess what it was? Nothing. It was empty. They felt better because they believed they were going to feel better. Several of them began to cry. They were actually pleased that their thoughts and not some random drug had been the key ingredient in their new sense of beauty.

One of my dear friends and fellow yoga teachers once told me that as she aged she was startled to see her mother every morning looking back at her from her bathroom mirror. Then one morning she woke up to find her grandmother looking back at her. She decided right then and there to put an end to that reflection. She did not go get a face lift, Botox, or any fillers. She did something a lot cheaper and probably much more empowering. She decided to greet her daily image with the phrase "Hello, beautiful." She said at first it was hard to say, but after a while she realized it was causing her to smile and she found it easier and easier, until she actually began to embrace it. When she writes me a note she always begins it with "Hello, beautiful." It makes me smile too.

"Beauty is only skin deep," "Don't judge a book by its cover," and "Beauty is in the eye of the beholder" are some of the adages about our outside appearance. The truth, however, is most of us live in a society that has a standard for attractiveness, and few of us are able to completely disregard how we are viewed. *The Twilight Zone* with Rod Serling featured an episode about a society that forced every young woman to choose a physical model from a menu of womanly styles when they reached the end of their teenage years. One young woman refused. She didn't want to look like everyone else. She liked herself the way she was, but this was not an option. She was forced to undergo the procedure. Her parents chose from the menu for her, and the powers-that-be took her away for the process. When the last scene is shown we see this Barbie-like woman looking in the mirror and being very pleased with what she sees. Yes, it was extremely disturbing, but like so much science fiction, it is becoming a present-day reality. I'm not against getting some "help" if that's what someone needs to do to feel better. As a cancer survivor I know the importance of looking good in order to feel good. My friend Greta Schiffman has presented the Look Better, Feel Better program to hundreds of women cancer survivors. The Duke Cancer Patient Support Program provides wigs, turbans, and prosthetics for cancer patients. There are times in our lives when we need to take a few extra steps to enhance our sense of well-being, and I belive that's just fine.

The lesson learned from the Dove beauty patch is fairly obvious; we can feel better about ourselves if we think differently. If we think we are beautiful, we will feel more beautiful. I'm not talking about a narcissistic obsession with ourselves. I'm talking about a healthy view and appreciation for who we are and how we look, regardless of another's opinion. We can decide to feel better by changing the way we think, by changing what we think. We aren't limited to our outer appearance either. How we choose and shape our thoughts affects every aspect of our lives. It affects our relationships, our work, our health, and our spirit. We get to choose what we want to focus on and what we want to believe about ourselves and the world, and with those choices, we determine the quality and maybe even the quantity of our lives. What's your choice? Do you want to look in the mirror and see ugly and sad? Or, like my dear friend, do you want to see happy and beautiful or, perhaps, handsome? Give it a try. "Hello, Beautiful!" or "Hi, Handsome!" Maybe you can avoid becoming a crazy robin and banging your head into something that won't ever make you feel better and only makes you feel worse.

9. Praying the Rosary

Affirmation: *I am committed to cultivating compassion for those who most need God's mercy.*

Many years ago when my husband Sandy and I were in New York City, we went to Ellis Island. The museum had recently opened and I was very eager to see it. I knew that both our ancestors had entered the United States through that terminal, and I felt it was an amazing opportunity to experience at least a trace of the United States' history in a very real way.

It was late when we headed off for the tour. It was a rainy, dark day. We stood in the line to embark on the ship and finally boarded and headed toward the island. It was remarkable! I was stunned by the size of the entry hall and took time to imagine what it would have been like to come into it, wondering if I would be allowed to enter the country or if I would be turned away. I could only imagine the exhaustion and anxiety that would accompany such an experience. We didn't have as much time as I would have liked because we'd started out so late, but I was pleased we had made the effort.

The last ferry was about to leave. It was still raining and now it was totally dark. We again waited in line to board the ship. When we finally got aboard, there weren't any seats but there was a little shelter toward the bow. My husband and I were quiet with our thoughts. I decided to say the rosary as we headed back to port. When you disembark the ship at Battery Park, there is not a queue for the taxis. One must search for transportation, and if you're trying to get back uptown it can be a daunting exercise. There weren't any taxis to be found anywhere. There were all these people vying for a ride and it was crazy! We decided to head off in the opposite direction of the crowd, to take the "path less traveled." As we walked along we were quiet and I threw in a few more Hail Marys. Roaming around that area in the dark was not our best choice, even for two streetwise people from NYC. We were becoming concerned when we turned a corner and two people were exiting a taxi.

We immediately got into it and took a few deep breaths. I don't remember the cabbie's name and why, you ask, would I? Well, the first thing we noticed is that he had on a classic music station, playing Pachelbel's Canon. I could feel the tension drain away, not only from me but from my husband, and then we both noticed the rosary hanging from the cabbie's rearview mirror. I smiled. I might have even giggled a bit. My husband turned in the seat and looked directly at me and said, "You've been praying the rosary, haven't you?"

Now, this was quite a while back. I say this because at this time if you hail a cab in New York, the driver probably doesn't speak English and they won't have music on. They have TV screens with advertisements that demand your attention, but even then, many years ago, most of the cabbies were from another country. The probability of getting an English-speaking driver was low. The probability of getting an English-speaking, rosary-practicing Catholic cabby was miraculous.

I have a young friend who is not a Catholic. She was raised a Christian but at this point her life had taken her in another direction. She shared with me that she was reading a book about Mother Mary, the goddess. It's not the first time someone has told me they thought of the Blessed Mother as a goddess. I once went for an interview for a graduate program and when I told the interviewer that I was a Catholic, she exclaimed, "Oh, that's so cool! Your faith has a goddess, Mother Mary." At that time I was surprised. So, I wasn't surprised this time. What surprised me is that my friend shared that she had begun to pray to Mary. She shared that she'd had an issue with a loved one who was not well and she didn't want to add to her relative's distress. Instead, she wrote a letter to Mary, burned it, and asked for peace. She was sharing with me that peace came, almost immediately, and it had remained with her.

Catholics are sometimes criticized for praying to others besides Christ. It's true we do, or I should say, I do. It's not that we're really praying to another. We're asking that spiritual being who we believe is closer to God at that moment than we are to intercede for us. I pray to St. Anthony, the patron saint of lost things, more and more often. It never fails! "Saint Anthony, Saint Anthony, please look around. I've lost my _____ and it needs to be found." I recite a lot of memorized prayers and several I've made up. I also pray the rosary. It was once explained to me that Mother Mary can intercede for us by asking for what we really need, many times when we don't ourselves have a clue what we really need.

It is part of the practice to meditate on one of the Mysteries of the rosary before beginning the prayers for each of the five decades of ten beads. There are four Mysteries, each one assigned to a different day or days of the week. They take you from the conception of Christ to the Assumption of Mary. I've been saying the rosary since I was a child and love to pray it, especially as I walk around our nearby lake. I find comfort in the recitation. With the reading of Father Haase's book, *Catching Fire, Becoming Flame*, I decided to make an effort to recite the rosary daily. He calls us to be of service. He reminds us that being of service is the purpose of our existence, and we are especially called to be of service to those most in need. I believe that to be true, and while I am a volunteer in many ministries, I wanted to do even more for the marginalized of society. I wanted to find a way to bring comfort and peace and hope to those most in need. I, therefore, have committed to saying the rosary daily for those God deems most in need of help. I believe in answered prayer. I achingly hope that my thoughts, intentions, and the energy I am sending forth into the universe are tenderly touching the lives of those who are suffering. I feel it's a step, perhaps the first step for me, toward feeling a greater sense of compassion for those who most need God's mercy.

If Mother Mary can bring peace to a nonbeliever and a New York taxi to a couple of nervous, wet, cold travelers, I am very hopeful about what she can do for the comfort of those who so desperately are in need of comfort. Join me. Pray *your* set of prayers for those who are suffering. Imagine our energy bringing solace, hope, maybe even joy to those who are suffering more than we can even imagine. Every thought we think, every word we say, every action we take affects everyone else in the world. May our thoughts and energy bring peace, salvation, and perhaps even joy to anyone in need of mercy.

10. Life Is a Banquet

Affirmation: *The world is an amazing place, and the more I learn about it and its inhabitants, the more I learn about myself.*

If you've ever been to Disneyland or Disney World, you've probably been to the Small World ride that plays the song "It's a Small World After All" over and over and over. My children always seemed to enjoy the ride, but after going on it just once, I found the song to be disturbing.

While traveling out of the country, I began to think about living in a small world. I once had a tour guide hand me extra passes to the Pope's Wednesday morning audience and say, "You never know who you'll meet. It's a small world, especially in Rome." In this instance, even with a million people there, I didn't meet anyone I knew. I must admit I have been very far from home when I've been stunned to meet someone from my local area. For the most part, however, I rarely meet an acquaintance when traveling. Mind you, I meet a lot of new acquaintances, just not a lot of known ones. And, isn't that one of the reasons to travel?

When my grandson Owen was thirteen, we went to London to visit with my adult daughter Ellen and her fiancé, Adam, and then Ellen, Owen, and I headed to Rome. I also took a similar trip with my granddaughter Isabelle when she was thirteen. After visiting London on that trip, we headed to Paris. Yes, I felt blessed to be able to share the world with them. I feel blessed that they wanted to come with me. As Isabelle and I deplaned in Raleigh and were heading toward customs, she asked me where we were going next. "We need to go through customs, honey." "Oh no, Grandma, that's not what I meant," and she smiled. Throughout this trip, Owen suggested I adopt a "travel buddy." He suggested himself.

When Ellen, Owen, and I were in Rome, the tour guide mentioned in passing that one corner shop had "the best gelato in Rome" and that the line for the gelato is sometimes longer than the line to enter the Vatican. When we finished our Vatican tour, I was ready to find our way back to our hotel and rest for a while, but that wasn't Ellen's plan. She whipped out her trusty iPhone and located that shop. We walked this way and that way, and what did we find? The best gelato shop in Rome. So there we stood in line with a group of nuns from Albania who had also discovered the shop. When they told us where they were from, Ellen surprised them by announcing she'd been to Albania. The nun told her to come visit the next time she had a reason to go there. We would have missed out on that whole experience if it wasn't for Ellen's desire to experience it all and to have gelato.

I have friends who have traveled all over the world. They aren't the least bit concerned with safety or, even worse, Montezuma's revenge, and if they are concerned, well, too bad. The adventure is more important than the worry. I think of them as having a huge appetite for life. They want to experience it all. They don't care if they encounter challenges along the way. In fact, they relish the challenges. Remember the movie *Auntie Mame* with Rosalind Russell? She says, "Life is a banquet and most poor suckers are starving to death." I don't want to starve to death. I, too, want to feast from the banquet of life.

What happens when one travels? Your world becomes larger. It's true, life is a banquet. There is such diversity, so many delightful flavors. I think that's why *The Amazing Race* has been one of my favorite TV shows. In it a dozen or more people travel around the world engaging in the local traditions and customs of the country they are visiting. What is of the greatest interest is not what they see or do, and I certainly don't recommend racing through any worthwhile experience. What is of the greatest interest is what happens to one's thinking when one steps outside of one's box. It's what happens inside us that's so amazing.

We get to choose whether or not we want to live inside a tiny little box, the known world, or expand the box. The world can be a scary place, but at some point we will no longer be a part of it. While we are here we should embrace the concept of living in a big space, of learning about our planet and its people and, therefore, about ourselves. It's too easy to stay safe and comfortable and to let our world shrink to our size. Maybe one doesn't really need to hop a plane or a train in order to stay green and growing. I have seen how small our world can become every time I visited an assisted living facility. We get to choose if we want to eat from a buffet or have the same food over and over. If travel is beyond your means, go to the library, go to the theatre, borrow some travel videos. There is no reason in this day and age to miss out on all that's available in the world that can nourish our minds, hearts, and souls and help us to live a life of abundance and adventure, even if we're confined physically by old age, illness, or finances.

Because of Ellen's sense of adventure, we got to meet Albanian nuns. How many people outside of Albania can claim that? Because of my sense of adventure, we got to go to mass in St. Peter's Basilica and view the Pieta and see Pope Francis. Owen's interests led us to see some of Banksy's London graffiti street art. Each of us journeyed to a new place. We discovered new people, new visions, new appreciations, and, therefore, we discovered more about both our outer and, most importantly, our inner worlds. I'm pleased my grandchildren and I have had the opportunity to travel together. This trip certainly wasn't the first, and the trip to Europe was the farthest but not, however, the longest. The longest journey is the one we take to know ourselves better, the one within, and by spending time together, especially in a foreign location, we learned a great deal about each other and about ourselves. We not only created some amazing shared memories, but we ate "the best gelato in Rome," we ate from the banquet of life, and it was great!

11. Journeying Through Motherhood

Affirmation: *Being a mother is my greatest joy.*

As we walked around the lake, the geese couple were crossing the path and next to them was a gaggle of goslings. The female goose raised her head and stared right at us, daring us to come closer. Behind us was another walker and her dog. The mother goose didn't hesitate. She took off charging, squawking loudly at the dog. It had come too close to her babies.

I'd been a mother for over forty years as of this writing. At this point I was also the grandmother of four great people. I was also non-biased. At one time my adult gym was offering toddler swim lessons on Saturday mornings. I felt a deep ache as I watched the parents interact with the children. I had an even stronger reaction when I saw the fathers caring for the little ones, holding out their arms for them to jump into and holding their little hands as they led them to and from the pool. I was nostalgic for that time but I remembered those lessons when I did them and then I realized I was just fine simply being an appreciative observer.

One day a young mother shared with a group of us that her fifteen-year-old daughter and husband had had their first terrible blowout. She was worried they would never have a trusting, loving relationship. The other mothers present assured her it was all normal growing pains, and if it had taken that long for them to have this type of interaction, they were probably going to be just fine, probably even better than fine.

Many years ago *The New York Times* ran an article about the happiness level of parents. The researcher reported that in general the parents of teenagers were unhappier than parents at any other stage. I don't remember being unhappy when my children were teenagers, but I do know that now that they are adults, I thoroughly enjoy their company and that of their spouses. It's pure joy when I have the opportunity to spend time with them. I think that what we spend our money on reflects what we consider to be important, and I'd rather spend my money on events that bring us all together than on anything else.

Today when I see a young family together, I want to run up to them and tell them it's a "short long journey." I want to embrace them and shake them and make sure they know it and tell them to savor every moment of it. Motherhood is work. It's painful and it's challenging. It's demanding and it's tiring. It's frustrating and it's confusing. As a young mother I was never around extended family. Our first move was when my oldest, Melissa, was six weeks old. Our second move five years later was when my middle child, Joey, was eighteen months old, and then ten years after that, we moved when Ellen was just three. I never had a support system. Every time we moved, I was completely on my own. At the time I didn't have a clue how very hard it was, but I fully recognize the difficulty in retrospect. Each time we moved, I had to create a new support system. It was easier sometimes than others. It was exciting to go to a new place, but it was also lonely. Our last move brought us here to North Carolina in 1986. We began again. At this time we live close to most of our family.

Also at the time of this entry, my oldest girl, Melissa, and her kind, loving husband, Larry, and my four grandchildren lived about two miles away. My son, Joey, and his beautiful wife, Belen, also lived close and I was blessed to still have my husband of forty-five years. My youngest and her sweet husband, Adam, were in London, and I was optimistic about the future.

My years of motherhood will never be over. Once a mother, always a mother, but this stage of being the mother of adult children was for me a rich blessing. While the children were growing, I was too busy with the cares of life and daily activities to savor all the precious moments they offered me. But now, I can relish each moment. I can relax in their company. When I was doing my MSW, I decided I would ask each of them, all adults at that time, how I did as a mother. Truly, this has been my life's work. I wondered how they felt I did. When I look back I remember each of their births. I remember all the times they were sick and needed care. I remember all those miles in the car to different sporting events or classes. I remember making dinner almost every night. I remember reading stories and grabbing hugs and kisses as often as possible. I remember helping with homework and visiting schools. I remember helping find colleges and going to ceremonies. I remember a home that I always hoped felt safe and secure. I welcomed their friends and eventually their spouses. I encouraged them to follow their dreams and listened when life went a different way. I hadn't had any training and other than my wonderful husband, I hadn't had any family around to guide me, but it appeared I'd done all right. What did they think? I was curious and I was brave.

Yes, it's been a "long short journey." If I could do it again, what would I change? If I were as wise at twenty, thirty, or forty as I am now, what would I do differently? I'd not clean the house so often. Occasionally I'd have cereal for dinner instead of taking time to cook each evening. I'd read even more stories, hold hands even more often. I'd sit and just listen whenever they wanted to tell me something. I'd know this moment would soon be gone and I'd treasure it for the gift it was.

They were kind to me when they answered my question. That response alone was an answer in itself. I'd done okay. I must have done okay. Sandy, my hubby, and I must have done well. They're still hanging out with us. In fact as I write this it's almost Mother's Day and the family and Sandy have gifted me with flowers, cards, a rice cooker, and most importantly, time together. Yes, I might change the way I did some things, go slower, be more mindful, but I wouldn't change choosing to be a mother, especially to these three remarkable people. I've been blessed and at least now I can go slower and relish each and every moment I get to spend with them.

12. Developing a Sense of Appreciation

Affirmation: *I have an attitude of appreciation for all things.*

The yoga class at Rex Wellness here in Cary had just begun when our teacher, Karin Johnson, invited us to "take an intention." She then suggested "appreciation."

It was spring of 2015 when I wrote this. The singing birds and flowering trees, bushes, and plants filled my ears with music and my vision with the color and the miracle of new birth. Life seemed to hold the promise of a joy-filled wedding celebration for my youngest daughter, Ellen, and her sweetheart, Adam O'Sullivan. We had been preparing and planning for the warm welcome and entertainment of our family, dear friends, and new family to be from all over the world. We had gifts, food, hugs, and smiles ready and waiting. My spiritual director, Sister Judy Hallock from A Place for Women to Gather, had also invited me to "take an intention." This time it was to be for the upcoming celebrations and to hold it for the events and for all those who would be involved in the celebrations.

When I spoke with Sister Judy about the upcoming wedding, I told her I was simply staying calm and allowing it to unfold in its own way. I was more than happy to be intimately involved in the support of the celebration, but both Sandy and I recognized that this was Ellen and Adam's wedding. We felt our role was to help them make their dream come true, not to force our preferences upon them, even if we could. Sister Judy, however, changed my focus. An intention of sitting back and letting the events simply unfold was not enough. She suggested I hold the week and all those who were helping us celebrate "in Divine Light."

I was ready for this guidance. I know about blessing events well before they begin. I've prayed for our Pink Ribbon Yoga Retreat, any workshops or classes I present, and all the communities in which I'm involved. I pray for the people individually and as a group. I pray for blessings and that the time spent is only to their benefit. I've done this for many, many years. I seldom enter an event I'm either responsible for or I'm simply a participant in without having held that event in prayer. Does it change how the event or the meeting goes? It changes it for me and I am sure I bring an attitude of joyful expectation rather than skepticism or worse, and that has to make a positive difference. Now, I was told I needed to do the same for the wedding of two of my favorite people. They'd been together for over fifteen years. My husband and I were overjoyed that they finally decided to make this public commitment to one another and to their world.

When Karin suggested we take "appreciation" as our intention, I wondered how that would be different from "gratitude," so I decided to give it a try. Later that day NPR had an interview with a man who had developed a mechanical spoon that allowed people to eat who had Parkinson's disease or any other tremor illness. It was explained that people with that type of condition cannot feed themselves. I had never thought about that disability. Immediately I remembered my intention from my class and appreciated the fact that I wasn't faced with that challenge. Recently I had also heard of Non-24, a disorder affecting the totally blind. It's a sleep disorder with which they struggle because they can't tell the difference between day and night. I wondered what other things I take for granted that may be a challenge for another? My appreciation of the lack of struggle my life presently holds instantly surged. I thought of all the friends and relatives I know about and for whom I am holding in prayer and was again appreciative. Really, when I look around the world and see what so many people have to deal with, I am in awe of the blessings of my life. I have no reason to complain or to be ungrateful about anything. It seems appreciation and grateful easily go together, and I just needed a boost. Karin's suggestion helped heighten my sense of gratitude.

By holding our upcoming celebrations in Divine Light, I found a heightened sense of appreciation and gratitude for these events and all the blessings I knew would emerge during this time. I also expected the weather to be perfect. I expected there to not be any glitches or bumps in the actual event. I expected all the guests would behave appropriately and there would be complete harmony among everyone in the family. Just teasing! What did happen because of my new intention was that I had a peaceful, joyful heart. I expected the best and was at peace with whatever that would look like. I wrote this entry with an anticipation filled with the excitement of the union of Ellen and Adam and of the blessings that would emerge from the union of our two families.

Thank you, Karin. Thank you, Sister Judy. Thank you, Loving God, for the gift of Divine Light. Your guidance helped me to experience and appreciate one of the most beautiful events of my life.

13. Claiming Your Power

Affirmation: *I did it!*

Graduations of all types have taken place at the time of year during which this is being written; celebrations of milestones, accomplishments, and dreams come true. My oldest granddaughter, Isabelle Bowling, graduated from the Raleigh Collaborative High School. It was a tiny school, only twelve children. There were only four students graduating. Our whole family attended the ceremony. It was a wonderful event. Two of the three teachers spoke, the principal spoke, Dr. Anderson, and each family had a family member (Isabelle chose her grandfather, my hubby) speak. Then, each student showed a slide presentation of their life and also gave a short speech. All of them were very nervous. There were about sixty people in the audience.

Isabelle was gracious in her talk, thanking her entire family for their support and including us and stressing how blessed she felt to be a part of such a loving family. We were so very proud of her accomplishments. My heart almost burst. She was the first presenter. The last student to speak was a young man, a man we knew to be twenty years of age, who was slight in stature and appeared very timid. He read his speech, hesitating over the pages and stumbling through several of the phrases. He ended and then he began to walk off the stage when he suddenly stopped and said, "Oh, I forgot something." He returned to the dais, looked out at the audience and especially toward his family, and raising his fist shouted, "I did it!" I wasn't the only person there with tears in my eyes. As I write this I still feel weepy with his joy of accomplishment.

My friend told me that when we arrive in heaven she thinks the question Saint Peter will ask us is "Did you appreciate and celebrate all God gave you? Were you joyful and grateful?" Was I? Have I been? Really? I began to journal. How many times in my life have I shouted, "I did it!" I have not, I have not claimed victory. I have downplayed my accomplishments more often than I have celebrated them!

As I wrote this I was in the process of preparing for an outward bound type of trip to the Kenai Peninsula in Alaska. Isabelle had been accepted to the Savannah College of Art and Design. It's the only school to which she applied, and she will be attending as a photography major. It is her passion. I was providing her the opportunity to photograph a part of the world which with neither of us was familiar. I was anxious. I'd been gathering all the gear necessary for this expedition, things I had rarely packed, if ever. I recognized I was blessed to be able to do this and to share this time with one of my favorite human beings, but it was way outside of my comfort zone and so I was quite nervous.

During 2016 I read Christiane Northrup's book *Goddesses Never Age.* Don't miss this book. I truly believe that any woman over the age of eighteen, maybe even younger, should be required to read this marvelous guide for a woman's life. If you don't get it and you're a woman reading this, at least turn the title into one of your affirmations and claim it! ***I am a Goddess!*** Toward the end of her book, in the middle of this trip's preparation, she wrote about the healing effects of being in nature.

Several of my readings, including Dr. Northrup's book, stressed the life-changing practice of letting go of our own agendas and attempting to live a life within the Divine flow. You've probably heard it, "Let go and let God." It's a lifelong practice. It takes patience and quiet and setting aside our egos. For me, it comes and I feel like I'm right there, following the "path" God seems to have laid out, and then I'm off doing my own thing again, taking back control of my life and truly believing I have control of it. Ha! What if, however, because of my time with the Lord, my prayer time and my meditation time, I was actually being led to this Alaskan experience? What if Alaska is a place where I would learn and grow and heal in a way beyond my wildest dreams? If I could have truly believed that, would I have been anxious or would I been excited?

After graduation and pondering the accomplishments of these four young people, I sat with my journal and wrote down several things in my life of which I feel very proud. I began with my education and then listed this wonderful family my husband and I have created. I went on to list several charity projects I've spearheaded and the positive, joyful manner in which I went through breast cancer. It wasn't a long list but I felt good about it. Then I sat back and I read it over. I read it again and I thought, *If I didn't know this woman and I read this list of accomplishments, I'd say,*

"Wow, this is a remarkable woman. I'd really like to meet her." Then, I thought of all the people in my life who, like myself, don't always see their amazing selves as others might see them. There are so many who don't really claim their accomplishments, especially the women.

My experience has led me to believe that most of us try to be humble and it's not always to our benefit. One of the young women from one of my study groups was sharing her accomplishments at work. She was effecting amazing changes in her workplace by guiding people toward a healthier lifestyle. She had engaged more people in this project than anyone else in her organization. She went on to explain why she was so much more successful than others. It wasn't because of her passion and knowledge. It was because the other counsellors were at some sort of disadvantage. "No, no, no," I said. "Claim it! You did it! You are using God's gifts to be the change people need. You are a remarkable woman." My other friend chimed in and said, "Don't bury your coins," or as Marianne Williamson says:

"Our deepest fear is not that we are inadequate. Our deepest fear is that we are powerful beyond measure. It is our light, not our darkness that most frightens us. We ask ourselves, Who am I to be brilliant, gorgeous, talented, fabulous? Actually, who are you not to be? You are a child of God. Your playing small does not serve the world. There is nothing enlightened about shrinking so that other people won't feel insecure around you. We are all meant to shine, as children do. We were born to make manifest the glory of God that is within us. It's not just in some of us; it's in everyone. And as we let our own light shine, we unconsciously give other people permission to do the same. As we are liberated from our own fear, our presence automatically liberates others."

What if each of us took some time to write down several things of which we are proud? I encourage you to do this exercise. Then read them like it's about someone you do not know. I'll bet you'll find yourself saying, "Wow! This is a remarkable person. I'd really like to meet her or him." I am expecting to add my Alaska outward bound trip to my list when Isabelle and I return, and with great joy and gratitude I will shout from the dais of my stage, "I did it!"

P.S. I did do it! It was the adventure of a lifetime. I am pleased and proud to shout, "We did it! I did it!"

SUMMER

1. Golf & Lessons Learned

Affirmation: *Every life experience leads to wisdom and knowledge.*

On June 19, 2011 Rory McIlroy won the US Open in golf. I am married to a golfer, and my adult son, Joey, took up golf after he gave up skydiving. (Thank You, Lord!) When I wrote this Sandy and I had been married for almost forty-five years and I had learned a lot about the sport. I had never considered myself a golfer, but at this point I had played golf for over forty years. Sandy has always been an amazing golfer. I always loved watching him play.

I used to resent his dedication to this pastime. When I had three young children, the time away from the family required by golf and desired by my husband was onerous for me. Then, however, when the children were grown and on their own, I could see the sport in a different light. Actually a few times over the years I might have even occasionally referred to myself as a "golfer."

Many years ago I read James Dodson's *Final Rounds*. It completely changed the way I saw the sport. It truly was a life-changing read. It helped, too, that my children were older and I had a little more free time. When I read the memories that he and his dad had collected together, I better understood the appeal of the game. Golf wasn't just "a good walk spoiled" as Mark Twain said; it was about so much more. It was about relationships and adventures and shared experiences. I took it to heart and started focusing on those aspects and not how many times I was hitting (or swinging) at that little ball. Yes, something changed. I started having more fun and truly valuing the time I spent with Sandy and with my son. Sometimes my daughter-in-law, Belen, joined us on the course as Joey's chauffeur. I really learned to value the experience.

Part of our shared interest lies in occasionally watching the major tournaments with my family. The US Golf Open is one of them. We found the 2011 US Open to be especially exciting. When Rory McIlroy won he was only twenty-two. He's from Northern Ireland. Not only did he win but he broke all sorts of records. He shot 65-66-68-68. He was as much as seventeen under par at one point. He went into the tournament winning by eight strokes. These accomplishments were unheard of.

That's all wonderful and exciting, but for me it was the story behind McIlroy's win that touched my heart. His father was there; it was his Father's Day present. The story that emerged was of a family of hardworking people. His dad had worked as a janitor, and when his son showed an interest in golf, he became the bartender at the golf club so that they could afford his lessons. When he accepted his award, he didn't leave out his "mum" either. He said it was because of their hard work and sacrifice that he was there that day.

Afterward, the media spent a great deal of time talking about this young man's loss at the 2010 Masters in Augusta. They kept talking about how he was winning by four strokes when the final round began, and then he "fell apart." Everyone was amazed that he had pulled himself together so quickly and was doing so well. Some had thought he might never recover from such a devastating loss. It was one of the questions presented to him several minutes after accepting the US Open trophy. The announcer asked him to speak about losing the Masters and what that had been like. Ready? "The Masters was a very valuable experience for me. I learned a few things about myself and my game."

One day when I went to play golf with the "big girls," the ladies who play golf often and for the most part quite well, I found I was way outside of my comfort zone.

Golf, yoga, and tennis are the three main physical activities in which I've participated. I think there's so much to learn about myself and sometimes others from watching the behavior that is exhibited during different events, especially golf. Concentration, perseverance, balance, forgiveness, humor, humility, and graciousness are required of the civil player, and many times, more than one aspect at a time is required.

The psychology of eighteen holes of golf is a microcosm of our lives. How do we interact with others? Are we kind, considerate, deferential, polite, encouraging? And how do we treat ourselves? Do we berate ourselves when we hit a bad shot? Are we annoyed when someone else does better? Can we focus regardless of what else is going on?

What are we thinking about? Is it lunch or dinner, or are we present to the experience? Do we notice not only the condition of the course but the topography, the fresh air, and the beautiful vistas?

Whatever we are doing on the golf course we are repeating in our daily lives. Our behavior toward others, ourselves, and the experience reflects our behavior through our lives.

Yes, it's the same in many sports. If you watch carefully, you'll see all your faults surface, but keep watching, be aware, and you'll be able to notice your strengths too. Perhaps it will be as simple as being able to share time with your loved ones, your buddies, a kind partner, and when asked how you played, even if the game didn't go as you had hoped, even though you didn't feel you played your best game, your answer will be "Wow! I had a great time!"

Rory McIlroy was much wiser than his twenty-two years. It takes some of us a lifetime to discover that every life experience leads to wisdom and knowledge. It's all up to us how we perceive it and whether or not we value every single one of them, both the accomplishments and the disappointments. Like Rory, it can lead us to championship skills, the skills of leading a rewarding, fulfilling life.

And, just in case you're curious, I played okay on that outing with the "big girls." I would even say, on that day, I was really and truly a "golfer" and I had a good time.

2. Overcoming Worry

Affirmation: *I let go of worry.*

She just announced she's going to Cuba. It's not her first trip. She's gone there before. My first thought is, *She is so brave.* My second thought is, *I hope she has a safe trip.* My third thought goes to my greatest fear: *I hope she's not abducted by a band of rebel guerrillas and made to traipse through the jungle where she gets all wrinkled and dies ugly.* Worry. I'm already worrying about her safety and, for that matter, my safety and I'm not even going.

My meditation reading this particular morning was from *Spiritual Insights for Daily Living*, edited by Elizabeth Fenske, and it was about worry. It said worrying about something was akin to having a headache and banging your head against a wall to get rid of it. I can be an active head-banger, but I have decided to stop worrying. Do you think that's possible?

The famous comedian George Burns once did a whole routine about worry. He said he gave up worry when he realized how futile it was. "It serves no purpose to worry about something you can't do anything about and if you're worried about something you can do something about, well, just go do it!"

My paternal grandmother developed Alzheimer's at a very young age. She died at the age of seventy-two. I believe the family first started to notice a change in behavior when she was fifty-five. I began worrying about getting Alzheimer's when I first heard it could be hereditary. I was in my early thirties. I even considered getting some sort of long-term care health insurance. I shared my concern with my young teenage daughter. Her response was "Oh, Mom, that's so silly. By the time you're that age, they'll have a cure for it." I stopped worrying. She was wrong, but it didn't matter. I was able to let it go for the time.

Worry can permeate our lives like a cancer, slowly growing without our ever recognizing the detrimental effect it is having. Not only does it undermine our sense of peace, but physically it causes the body's sympathetic nervous system to release stress hormones such as cortisol, which is harmful to our immune system. It is natural to be concerned about our lives, but there is a difference between concern and obsession. Once we become obsessed with a concern, we are in a place that won't allow us to clearly view our situation, and we become muddled. It truly is a useless exercise, wasting so much of our precious energy. Sometimes, however, all the positive thinking in the world will not decrease your anxiety. One anxiety related condition is known as generalized anxiety disorder, and it is treatable with medication and cognitive behavioral therapy. Anxiety is not always just in our mind; sometimes it's chemical and in order to turn things around, one may need some additional assistance.

In 2013, a meteor the size of a school bus—10,000 tons with the power of an atomic bomb—landed in Russia. A number of people died. There were numerous videos of it streaking across the early morning skies. It appears all the cars in Russia have cameras on them to record accidents, designed to act as a third, impartial witness. I couldn't help wonder how many people that day were worrying about an asteroid landing on them. We can worry about things that probably will never happen, and if we knew what was going to happen, we'd be worried all the time. In my husband's book, *Humanity at Work,* he tells the story of the fish and the pelican. There's the fish swimming along watching out for the barracuda or some other predator when along comes a pelican and swoops it up, a creature from another universe totally foreign to the fish's world.

We have no idea what life is going to present to us, a meteor or perhaps a pelican. I felt like a meteor landed on my life when I was diagnosed with breast cancer in 1999. I know I speak for many when I say that many of the physical diagnoses we receive come as total shocks. Sometimes they are conditions about which we have never even heard. We may not even be able to pronounce them or perhaps we have heard about them but never considered they would affect us. Truly, if we really wanted to worry all the time, I'm sure we could make up lots of stuff. Actually, most of our worries are fantasy driven because we can never know what the future will bring; we can only guess. Let go of your concerns for the future, and focus on the now.

This is one of the wonderful side effects of prayer and meditation. When we have a practice that brings us back to the present, we can use it in times of concern to recognize we have jumped off into the unknown and to bring ourselves back to the here and now. Prayer and the belief in a benevolent God can bring great peace.

In *Conversations with God*, Father Francis Fernandez addresses the passage from the Bible, Matthew 6:34, *Do not be anxious about tomorrow, for tomorrow will be anxious for itself. Let the day's own trouble be sufficient for the day.* He goes on to say, "What matters is today. Worry magnifies the difficulties and diminishes our ability to fulfill the duty of the present moment. We can live only in the present. Anxieties almost always arise because we fail to put all our effort into the here and now." If we believe we will be given the graces we need in order to contend with anything that crops up, we will be victorious!

Perhaps with continued practice, I will let go of worry. Perhaps I will even be able to celebrate in my friend's trip to Cuba and, instead of feeling anxious about it, send her along with heartfelt blessings and a vision of a wonderful adventure.

3. Carpe Diem

Affirmation: *This is the day The Lord has made, let me rejoice and be glad in it. (Psalm 118:24)*

Benjamin Franklin said, "The only things certain in life are death and taxes." I'm sure there are those who hope to avoid taxes; I would imagine most get caught. Willie Nelson and Al Capone come to mind. Some others, however, don't make enough money to have to pay taxes, and that seems very sad to me. When it comes to death, however, no one, I repeat, no one gets out of it. There is no avoiding it; we are all caught in the end.

It seems to me that many people, especially here in the West, believe if you don't think about death, it won't happen. Certainly it's one of our greatest fears—it's the greatest unknown. Those who have a faith have reasons to believe in an afterlife, and that can bring a great deal of comfort. I, myself, have chosen that belief, but I haven't met anyone who has returned from the great unknown. I do know one or two people who have had near-death experiences, and from what I've read that is usually a very positive experience. But other than the tales I've read about people who claim to have had life-after-death events, I can't claim any personal experience. I guess part of the good news is those who have those experiences report *something*, not a total void, not complete nothingness. In *The Naked Now*, Richard Rohr shares his belief that our spiritual development here on earth will determine our after-death experience. He says that the relationship we've developed with God here on earth will be the relationship we have after death. I once had a dear friend tell me she thought Christians would be met by Christ, Muslims by Allah, and Buddhists (even though they don't believe in an afterlife) Buddha. Does that mean an atheist is met by no one?

Death was very prominent in my life during the first half of 2014. I lost my mom, Margaret Grolimund, in March of that year, which was difficult, but much of my life's work has revolved around supporting people in crisis. The two Duke advisory boards I have sat on are both for cancer programs. The Duke Cancer Patient Support Program is for the patients and families of cancer patients, and the other is the Preston Robert Tisch Brain Tumor Advisory Board. My passion for the Pink Ribbon Yoga Retreat for women breast cancer survivors brings me in contact with many people challenged by cancer; I sing for my church's Resurrection Choir during the funerals; and I belong to two prayer groups. I don't know if you know this, but most prayers on a prayer list are not of praise and thanksgiving; they are prayers for the healing, peace, and comfort of the afflicted. At times I've been overly blessed with requests for prayers for a lot of people who are faced with serious, life-threatening challenges.

Even though at this time I had practiced yoga for over forty years, I had never given too much thought to the final resting pose, Savasana or in English, Corpse Pose (resting on your back, eyes closed). When I attended the Raleigh Yoga Fest, one teacher told us that Corpse Pose has that name because it can bring the concept of death to our attention. At the end of our practice she instructed us to imagine we were dying, to imagine letting go of Everything. She presented it as an opportunity for growth and awareness. It was a powerful exercise for me. It made the rolling over to one side into a fetal position before coming to a seated position even more meaningful. My practice took me from death into rebirth. I was beginning again, a new start, and that's what I believe death is. It's a new beginning, hopefully for me with Christ as promised. Even if I'm practicing, I'm not ready. However with all of the news I'd been receiving, I became even more aware of how precious every day is.

Let's admit it, we may be only one breath away from this life and the next. I cannot tell you how many people have come into my life who have had a prognosis of less than a month to live. These people were not ill. They just started feeling yucky, finally went to get it checked out, and boom, they were given the news that they were terminal! It's really scary. I know we have no way of knowing when our final day will occur. Sometimes there's absolutely no warning. I heard a tale about a man who went to market in Samaria and returned ashen. When he was asked what was wrong, he shared that he had had a brush with death. He asked a friend if he could borrow his horse so he could get away and go to Baghdad. His friend obliged him and then went to the market to see what was going on. When he arrived he ran into Death and asked him why he was looking for his friend. Death said that he wasn't looking for the friend. He was simply surprised to see him in Samaria because he had an appointment to meet him tomorrow in Baghdad.

Ever since my dad, Frank Grolimund, died in 1980 when I was only thirty-four, I've tried not to waste a day. I became very aware of the preciousness of each and every day. It's a meditation, however, and I'm not always present to it. But after these last experiences, and especially during this time, I was even more aware of how important it was to enjoy every day to the fullest. I even went and ate McDonald's french fries one day for lunch, which for me was very daring. This is it! Seize it! Live it! Be joyful in it, count the blessings, be grateful for what is and what is not. Do not utter a complaint or a criticism. Look around, recognize what truly is a problem and what are "ha ha" problems—those problems most of the world wishes they had—and then give praise and thanksgiving. Go ahead, eat dessert first, and even more important, tell your loved ones how you feel. Don't let the day slip away without living it and sharing it to the fullest.

4. Being of Service

Affirmation: *I believe that my prayer to help someone in need is always answered and is supported by God in ways that are beyond my wildest imaginings.*

In the book *The End of Your Life Book Club* by Will Schwalbe, he tells the story of his mother's life. The story revolves around her battle with pancreatic cancer and their journey through her treatment and, as you can figure out from the title, her death. They are a two-person book club with either the advantage or disadvantage, depending upon your view, of not having to provide food for the attendees. They read and discuss a long list of books over the two-year period of her treatment. It appears they have always been a two-person book club but didn't "officially" establish it until they were sharing her final challenge. It's cleverly written in that with each book they read, Will Schwalbe not only writes about the book but about his mother's life. I made a list of each of the books with the intention of reading some of the ones they shared. Some of them I'd already read. I also knew, however, that I'd be skipping some of his recommendations. They are way too disturbing for my taste. Just listening to the struggles of the protagonists on their reading list was enough to remind me of how cruel the world and fate can be.

Will is a publisher at the beginning of the book. His mother was an activist and a heroine. She was in her seventies at the time of her diagnosis and had been a first for women in many areas. For example, she was the founding director of the Women's Refugee Commission. She was an advocate for women and children refugees all over the world, and she'd traveled to many of those areas. You can Google her or read the book if you'd like more information. Her final project was to build a library in Afghanistan, and she wasn't going to die until that was accomplished. It was built. I guess she was a lot like Angelina Jolie, just not a famous celebrity. I also have the impression she didn't have the protection, guidance, or ease of travel given to a movie star. She was in the trenches with those who most needed help. Mary Anne Schwalbe was a courageous and compassionate woman. Her whole life, regardless of the danger or difficulty, revolved around being of service to others.

This was a good book for me. I live a blessed life of comfort, and the older I get, the more I seem to gravitate toward being comfortable. That includes an element of safety. I have not traveled to "dangerous" places, at least as far as I believe. I know going around the block can sometimes be dangerous. I have, however, been working at seeing the broader, worldwide picture of those in need. I know there are people suffering in ways I cannot even imagine and don't want to imagine. My husband, Sandy, and I sponsor several children in different programs around the world. We've always contributed to our church's appeals and those of nations who suffered natural disasters, and we make every effort to reach out whenever we are directly faced with a need with which we can assist. Our church, St. Michael the Archangel, has a sister parish in Honduras which we support, and more recently we reached out to a charity in Tanzania presented to us by St. Bernadette Church in Linville, NC. We've also supported Oie Osterkamp's Sharefish organization, which does work with the poor in Honduras. Last year, after I read Fr. Albert Haase's *Catching Fire, Becoming Flame* in order to do something more, I added praying the rosary for those "most in need of God's mercy." It allowed me to stay safely in my comfort zone and yet to become more sensitive and aware of the world's plight. (See the Spring entry, Praying the Rosary.)

I'm sharing these examples to illustrate that I've really tried to be more "world conscious." I try to stay informed but not overly concerned because I feel I only have so much energy, and some days just caring for myself and my family is all I feel I can do. Let's face it, the world is a very big place and here I sit, one of billions of beings. What kind of a difference can I make? Yet, when I read about people like Mary Anne Schwalbe, I wonder what more can I do? What else can I add to my efforts that might bring comfort, peace, hope, and even joy to those suffering on this planet?

One of my study groups read Anthony DeStefano's *Ten Prayers God Always Says Yes To*. One of the first prayers he offers is "Please use me to help someone in need." I hesitated. My initial reaction was to back away. I fully recognized this was a prayer God would not deny, but what would be required of me in order to follow His will? Would I be asked to travel to a third-world country undergoing revolution or one that had just experienced a devastating weather event? Would I be asked to give up all I had, like the young man in the New Testament, and follow God to poverty and perhaps martyrdom? Perhaps even worse would be if more and more was added to my already full plate, and in an effort to be of greater service to the world, I became neglectful of where my true service lies—my family and my community. I could immediately see all the pitfalls of such a prayer, and yet I felt ready to step out in faith.

I said the prayer. I'd been saying it for several weeks and as I journaled I found myself relaxing in the prayer, relaxing in my belief that if I'm called to do God's work, to be of more service to those in need, God will provide the support to do just that. I stepped out in faith. I believe that through prayer not only will I be of greater service but that I will be given the discernment to know which requests are from God and which are of my ego. I believed deep breaths, quiet time, and prayers from the depth of my heart would lead me where I was most needed. Yes, it could be to some third-world country. I trust God will come with me there, too. It could also be to a place I haven't yet examined, a place within, which takes me to a marvelous place not so far from where I am now but enables me to see it in a different light, a light of service right here and right now.

What do you think? Are you willing to step out in faith? Go ahead, say it: "God, please use me to help someone in need." I hope you'll let me know what you discover.

5. Shame on You

Affirmation: *I release myself from shame.*

"Shame on you!" This phrase can sometimes be accompanied by an accuser wagging his or her index finger at you while they are saying it. "Shame on you!" Does anyone use that phrase anymore? I hope not but whether it's said or not, many people carry around a deep sense of shame even if they don't understand its meaning. During this time my study group was reading *Daring Greatly* by Brené Brown, and one of her main topics is shame.

Is shame different from guilt? Can it possibly be a useful emotion, one that might help someone become healthier and more productive? Could it possibly help someone at least become kind and compassionate? No, I don't believe it helps in any way.

In fact, when I Googled it, one of the phrases used to describe shame was an "unhealthy emotion." I think when someone is pointing their finger at you and saying, "Shame on you," it's no different from them cursing you and telling you, "Go to hell!" There is no redeeming value in their condemnation. They are condemning you as a person; they are not condemning your behavior, and that's where the difference comes in between shame and guilt.

Shame is when you feel like you are unworthy because you believe there is something inherently wrong with you; you are a bad person. Guilt is when your behavior is faulty and because of it, because of your humanity, you've made a mistake, you've done something wrong. Unfortunately, it doesn't have to be someone other than ourselves pointing that finger. Many of us are adept at saying, "Shame on me!" That, too, is not doing anything to help you create a better life. One needs to fully comprehend the difference between believing one is inherently evil and that one has done an evil thing and can make amends and go on to change one's behavior.

I believe many people suffer from shame because of what they were told as a child by a parent, teacher, or some other misguided authority figure—or even worse, something that was done to them as a child.

Those who make it to adulthood and don't suffer from the malady of shame are either completely skewed or had some wonderful people in their lives who with their affirmations diffused those who attempted to harm them. They gave them the gift of discernment. I've had many people tell me their religion made them feel worthless and shameful. I can see how that might happen, but at some point don't you think you have to shuck off that mantle and decide what empowers you and what is hurting you, instead of blaming it on something in your past? How is that done?

That's why I began to write, to give people the opportunity to think about their beliefs and whether or not those beliefs are enhancing their lives or diminishing their lives. When I was discussing this specific topic with a friend, she told me SHAME was an acronym for "should have already mastered everything." I don't think she was talking about our hobbies, although I believe how we approach our hobbies is a reflection of how we feel about the more important aspects of our lives, like our faith and our relationships.

Perfectionism is the birthplace of shame. We may have a belief system that has led us to a point where we expect so very much from ourselves. There seems to be a fine line between expecting to do something perfectly and setting the bar so low that we never excel at anything. If you've read any of my previous writings, you know that at one point I raised the bar on both my golf game and my fiddle playing. There's no way to keep score for fiddle improvement, so since I'd practiced almost daily, I gave myself credit for improving. Golf, however, is very different. Each swing—no matter how big or small, near or far—counts equally. Gauging my improvement or lack thereof is easy.

Soon after writing the *Golf and Lessons Learned* entry, but after some additional practice and a lesson, I headed out to play with "the big girls." What a lesson in life for me… I was abysmal! Notice the phrase carefully. I didn't write, "My game was abysmal." I fully felt like there was something inherently wrong with me. When describing my experience to a dear friend and lifelong golfer, I was hoping for some great insight to dispel how embarrassed and actually ashamed I was by my performance. In retrospect, I am so grateful to have had this experience. It was nonthreatening, even trivial in some way, but because I'd been studying *Daring Greatly*, it gave me a great opportunity to see how I can point that finger of shame at myself and suffer that unhealthy emotion.

My friend and her husband said all the right things. There they were, the people we all need in our lives to lift us up and affirm our personhood. I wasn't being silly. "It was easy to beat ourselves up over our performances." They had had exactly the same experiences. With their encouragement and a few more lessons from my coach and number one fan, my husband, Sandy, I took the lessons of golf and life that I had just learned and headed out to play once again. I once again headed out with a new attitude. I would do my very best, and no matter what, I would have fun. I would enjoy my time. I would not beat myself up. I felt differently and I think that alone helped me play better, a life lesson for me. Do my best and choose to enjoy whatever I'm involved with. And, when I'm shamed either by myself or another, take it to those who love me and let them help lift me back up to a place of light and joy.

Shame is a disease of the spirit, not the mind. This is probably why religion has been so successful at using shame as a tool to control its flocks. We don't need to be reminded of our sinful nature; most of us are very aware of our imperfections. What we really need is encouragement and healing. That, too, is available through most faiths. Unfortunately, we must sift through the fire and brimstone to find it, but it is there. That's where the healing is too. It's in the attention to spirit. In fact, I firmly believe once we ask for healing, the Universe will gather all its forces to begin the process and will come to us in ways in which we never even dreamed.

I am a great believer in the Holy Spirit. Oh, I am sure there are many, many names given the Holy Spirit by all those who believe there is a power greater than anything of which we have an inkling. Give it any name you like. It's that life force that penetrates the very core of every living thing. It's available to all of us, but most of us are simply too busy or too thick to notice it. When we sit in silence and invite Divine Energy into our lives and our beings, miracles occur. Healing occurs. This is the antidote to shame. We invite God into every cell of our beings. We are part of the Divine. It is our birthright to share in the holiness and glory of God. Once we acknowledge our connection and our heritage to God's Divine gifts, healing begins.

6. Listening to God

Affirmation: *I believe in answered prayer.*

Buddy was a Brittany—not a Brittany spaniel, which is a common mistake because the breed looks like a spaniel, somewhere between a cocker and a King Charles. They are, however, their own special breed, and special was Buddy. He was orange and white, and as far as we were concerned, he was the most beautiful dog ever, inside and out.

I was searching for a new dog. We'd had dogs most of our lives and at the time we only had Misty, our cat that had adopted us a few years earlier. She was only allowed in the garage because the children were allergic to cats. That lasted about a month, and eventually she ruled the entire house whether people were sneezing or not.

This time I was determined to get a dog that was appropriate for our family. We hadn't always been successful with our adoptions. Ralph was a prime example. He was a hyper Dalmatian who consumed a picnic table, did several thousand dollars' worth of damage to one of our cars when he wanted to get in and play with the children, and sprayed all the furniture to insure that his territory was marked. After a year or so we were able to find a farmer who wanted to care for him. It had been a very trying experience. He wasn't the only dog with which we had issues, and I was hesitant to take on another pet with which I might fail. I am not the best "dog person." I might as well admit it. I am not a Cesar Millan, the dog whisperer. I'm not sure I have a single gene that enables me to respond appropriately to a dog's deepest desires. I'm a good caregiver, please understand. I feed, shelter, offer warm, cozy beds and long walks and good medical care. I even undergo lots of training sessions, but I can't seem to hear their innermost concerns. It didn't matter with Buddy. Perhaps one of the reasons we did better with him was because he came to us at eleven months of age and was already somewhat trained. Or maybe it was because I had asked God whether or not to adopt him, and God had sent a very clear message.

When I "found" Buddy, I sat quietly to pray about adopting him. I don't know what I expected, but I'd read a lot about praying for specific answers and I was desperate. I didn't want to disappoint another animal with my inability to create a livable space for it and for the family. I was afraid. I prayed, "God, what should I do? Should I allow this animal to come into our home?" and then I waited. I was prepared to wait for as long as it took. It wasn't more than a couple of breaths when I "heard," "It won't be easy, but it will be worth it." I was stunned, but there it was, my answer. I stood up, called the breeder, and a week later Buddy was being delivered to us by the New Jersey breeders who *happened* to be driving to their new home here in North Carolina. It was destiny. I'm here to tell you, God was right. I had my struggles but it was really, really worth it. Buddy lived with us for fourteen years, and he was the best dog ever. When I shared this tale, Buddy had been dead for six years, but we still had his ashes and his photo in our bedroom! I cried as I wrote this. I know many of you completely understand.

My friend Mary Ann Scope put down her English bulldog and longtime friend in 2015. That's what prompted this story. She said she cried for days; she's probably still crying, like me. My other friend Tracie Barton-Barrett has written a book about grieving for our pets, *Buried Deep in Our Hearts*. It's a reality, isn't it? There are so many life lessons we experience through our non-human companions. The most important lesson being that of unconditional love. I have one photo of Buddy where he had gathered all of my sneakers. He had a "soft mouth" because he was a bird dog. He dropped them all around his bed and then snuggled in for a nap.

My husband, Sandy, loves to tell the story about when I was gone for six weeks doing my yoga training at Kripalu. Buddy waited outside the back door, in the garage, every day until I finally returned, He had slept with Sandy every night in our bed until the night I came home, when he wouldn't come up on the bed even when called. He was just fine going back to his own bed next to ours. I was home and he was good again. Amazing!

Sandy shared his tiny family home with a dog named Missy. She was a Doberman they found in their backyard. She was very protective of that family! One day when he went to see his father's office, he was struck by the fact that the only picture Joe, his dad, had on his desk was of the dog. He asked where the other family photos were, and his father told him, "Missy is the only one that runs to the door to greet me when I come home." There it is again, unconditional love, total devotion; all the qualities we wished we and our loved ones emulated.

There have been hundreds of doggie movies about their journeys around the globe in an effort to return to their owners. One we watched is *Red Dog*, an Australian film about a dog and his deceased owner. It's a great example of how much they love us and affirm us regardless of who we are or how dumb we are.

My adult daughter Melissa and my granddaughter, Isabelle, have volunteered over the years at the Wake County SPCA. They are "dog people." They always have at least two dogs in their home. One day they brought home Gibson, a six-week-old mixed breed. What joy! Gibson discovered a pincushion on the top of the dining room table. He didn't eat it, but he did eat the thirteen pins and one needle. Their rescue dog needed several thousand dollars of surgery. They were saving for a new roof but their priorities were with this new guy who brought smiles and giggles and, once again, the unconditional love of a pet.

As I write this we are "pet free," but I am beginning to open my heart and mind to maybe adopting another dog—maybe! I haven't found one yet who is asking to come here. Once again, however, if one does come a knocking, I plan to sit with God and find out what the message is for us. It won't surprise me at all if once again I am told, "It won't be easy, but it'll be worth it."

7. What Was I Thinking?

Affirmation: *I carefully choose my thoughts.*

The 2013 Pink Ribbon Yoga Retreat had just ended. It was our ninth retreat. You can gather more information about it from the website PinkRibbonYoga.org. The retreat provides women breast cancer survivors with support, coping skills, and relaxation. It is designed to be both nurturing and empowering. What happens over four days and three nights? Miracles happen.

In 2013, twenty-nine people attended the retreat. We always take an intention to guide our planning, and our intention for this year's retreat was "On Wings of Joy." We borrowed a thousand paper cranes from the Duke Cancer Patient Support Program and hung them from the rafts. Yun Soho, one of our committee members and gifted artist, created mobiles for everyone. She hand-folded five paper cranes for each attendee and then added a hand-cut card from which they hung. Along with Irene Talton, our other gifted artist and yoga-off-the-mat instructor, they crafted inspirational words on the top of each mobile.

The retreat follows a very specific format. It's proven to be extremely beneficial for creating a healing environment for each individual and for the group as a whole. Over the years we've discovered that if we provide a single meaningful word for each person, they are more comfortable speaking in our opening circle. This year we used the words on the mobiles to initiate sharing. We then left the mobiles hanging on the back of the chairs and reused them for our closing circle. I think only one person got the same word for both circles, and that was me. It was "healing."

Healing is one of the miracles that takes place during these four days. I know because I always come away feeling healed. I like to hope that it's a complete healing from all my ailments—mind, body, and spirit—but I don't know that for sure. There certainly could be some rebellious cells floating around inside, although I hope not. I do know, however, that I come away feeling rested, valued, calmer, centered, nurtured, and empowered. I know, too, that all those positive emotions can lead me, my body, to a place of better physical health, and even if I am not cured of all my ailments, I know I am healed. There is a difference and I know I am not alone. I know it because over the last several years, the women who have participated in the retreat have told me so. It is true.

The very first thing we do when the retreat starts is to provide an atmosphere of safety. We encourage everyone to respect the confidentiality of any sharing that takes place. We ask that only one person speak at a time and that everyone else simply listens. We ask that each person use the word "I," not "you" or "we." We let everyone know that sharing is optional and that silence is not only accepted but valued. Before the next person begins speaking, the last person must declare that they are "complete."

We tell everyone that this is their time, all four days and three nights. We have all sorts of wonderful offerings, but their first responsibility is to take care of themselves, and so if they need to take a walk or a nap or to just have some quiet time, then that's what they should do. Of course, if they want to do yoga on the beach, try creating a watercolor of spirit, participate in yoga dance, eat ice cream with the group, try the meditation sessions, or experience laughing yoga, they are welcome to join in. One other thing that quickly becomes apparent is the lack of judgment that permeates the event. For at least a short while no one has to hide whatever might cause one to be embarrassed in the outside world. With that, the women can simply be. There is no striving, no pretending. It's liberating. It's another modality that promotes healing.

One of our traditions is to jump into the ocean after the early morning yoga. There's something magical about floating on the warm waves early in the day with a group of friends. One morning I was quite tired and I thought maybe I'd skip the swim and just head back to breakfast, but I wore my swimsuit just in case. The yoga ended and several ladies headed toward the water. I joined them. As I floated over and through the gentle waves, I couldn't imagine what I had been thinking that would have kept me from this amazing ocean experience. And then I realized, I often find myself in really neat situations that I was initially hesitant to join. Sometimes they involve big steps, like when I joined my daughter-in-law and traveled with her to Ecuador, and other times, they're small steps, like jumping into the ocean. Each time, however, I find myself wondering, *What was I thinking?*

Perhaps if we paid close attention, we'd discover that most of the time we're not very clear about what we really want or what will make us happy or perhaps what our best choice is. An example would be when we choose to have that second helping of something that tasted really good but is not good for us. How often have any of us done that and then shortly afterward wondered, *What was I thinking?* It would be wonderful to always be clear about our decisions, to always be mindful, but it's a practice, a lifelong practice. We can only stay alert and be aware.

After the retreat is over, I find myself asking that same question about having this idea of a yoga-beach retreat for women breast cancer survivors: *What was I thinking?* What made me think it would become a reality? Did I believe that it would turn into such a powerful, healing experience for so many people? Where would the money come from so everyone could afford to attend? Where would we find a place to stay? Who would volunteer to be our teachers? How would we advertise? There were dozens of questions and challenges to making this a reality. What was I thinking? I was thinking this was a good idea, and if I moved forward and it didn't happen, well, at least I tried. It's better to try and fail than to never try at all, but it didn't fail. It happened. It happened and it has provided comfort and healing, support and respite to more people than I had ever imagined. What was I thinking? I don't really know what I was thinking, but I do know I'm really glad and actually very proud that I was thinking at all. I'm thrilled that the retreat exists and that because of the work of so many wonderful people, we achieved the creation of such an amazing, awesome experience.

When I wrote this it had been over a week since the retreat took place, and I am pleased to say I was still floating on the "wings of joy."

8. Peace Be with You

Affirmation: *Peace begins with and within me.*

Once upon a time an amateur golfer could purchase hole-in-one insurance. If the golfer made a hole-in-one, he or she would receive an all-expense paid trip to anywhere in the world. I knew this because one of my husband's business associates at that time had just returned from a trip to Hawaii that he had "won" through this program. My husband had a birthday coming up and I thought this would be an excellent present for him (for us!). I probably had a slight attack of conscience because I mentioned it to him to make sure this was something he'd really enjoy. He would not, he told me. What he really wanted was a new set of golf head-covers. That's what I bought him. He was happy.

The following week my husband had his second hole-in-one. It did not make him happy. He certainly didn't want to call me to tell me about it. I think if he could have kept it from me for the rest of his life, he would have, but we lived in the tiny town of Norwich, New York, and word would reach me probably sooner than later. As you can imagine I was very disappointed. I can think of several things I might have done differently had I known he was to have this hole-in-one after telling me not to buy him the $40 hole-in-one insurance. But it's always easier in retrospect, isn't it? We're always so much wiser in retrospect, aren't we? What would life be like if we were people who knew ahead of time what was going to happen?

I love those sci-fi movies about time travelers. I especially like the ones where people go back to the past. Two of my favorites are *Back to the Future* with Michael J. Fox and *Peggy Sue Got Married* with Kathleen Turner. In both films they were able to impart helpful knowledge to people in their past to help them improve their lives in the future. In *Peggy Sue*, Kathleen Turner has a nerdy friend who believed her story that she was from the future. He wanted to know what he should invest in. "Panty hose," she suggested.

What should I invest in now that will insure my future success? Do I need to be able to see the future to make those decisions? Maybe I would be able to pick out the winning Powerball number or I could buy some sort of unknown stock, like Apple, before it went through the ceiling. Perhaps one would know who not to marry or what job not to pass up. Oh, the places one could go and the things one could do without any concern, without any confusion.

I have several dear friends whose early married lives were very difficult. One friend's husband left her with three children and declared bankruptcy. Right after he left, her house burned to the ground. These were only a few of the challenges she faced at that time. Her husband then began a new relationship and a new business, and she was left to figure out how to survive. The really good news is she did more than survive—she thrived!

It's been a few decades now since my friend experienced all this, but several years ago she found out her ex-husband was dying. She held a lot of justified resentment toward him, but she picked up the phone to talk to him and instead of venting all her frustration and anger, she found herself thanking him. For what? For her three wonderful children, for her stamina and fortitude, and for the life she was living. If she could have seen into the future with all the travail she would face, she probably would have still chosen the same; a different choice would have meant she would be a different person, and she's a marvelous human being because of the trials she's overcome. She has made peace, not only with her ex-husband, but with life.

In the Catholic mass we have one phrase that is used three times. "Peace be with you." Three times the priest says, "Peace be with you." No other phrase is repeated even once, but this one is repeated three times. Why? Because it's the one gift everyone desires: peace. When we are in the middle of war, most of the population want it to end. They want peace. When we are in the throes of caring for someone in pain, we pray for their peace. When someone has experienced the death of a loved one, we ask for them to have peace. When we or someone we know is faced with any sort of difficulty, financial or physical, we want to see them come to a peaceful place.

Peace. What does it look like? Can one find it in any situation? Recently, an acquaintance confided that his job might be at risk. We reacted with alarm. He, on the other hand, told us he wasn't worried. There was nothing he could do about it right then, so he wasn't upset. He was at peace. We may not have a definitive definition for peace but we all know when it's missing. We all know when we are not at peace. It is one of God's greatest gifts. We can claim it whenever we want. Once we are at peace with ourselves, we can radiate that peace out into the rest of the world.

It might seem like foreknowledge might be a better gift than peace, but it doesn't matter. There is no such thing, no matter what the psychic tells us. There's no guarantee that we'll ever know what the future will hold. But, we can find peace with whatever life has brought us. We can let go of the disappointments, the trials, the hurts, the not-so-wise choices, and we can ask God to let us go forward with the gift of peace. We can go forward knowing that our lives—the good, the bad, and the ugly—are exactly as they are supposed to be and that with God's gift of peace, we can rest in all of it.

9. Treasuring the Earth

Affirmations: *I treasure our planet Earth and recognize my responsibility to care for it.*

Carolyn Tobin was the presenter for the program titled "Sacred Time," but the topic on which she spoke was broader and deeper than that of time. I didn't think that was possible, but I was wrong and I was immediately enamored with her subject. She was there to speak about saving the human race, saving the universe, and saving ourselves. I was ready! Tell me there's a way to help in this most important work and I shall do my part, although I was doubtful about what I, one little lady living in the comfort of North Carolina, could possibly do that would help save mankind or womankind. Once again, I was being challenged to rise up and exert whatever power I did have to make a difference in this frightening world of ours. This same topic of making a difference in the world had appeared numerous times over the last few weeks, actually over the last couple of years. I was being led to *do more* or at least to *do something*. What was Carolyn offering me that would enable me—no, empower me—to heal the world?

Carolyn was a student of Thomas Berry, and she had recently published a book about their conversations, *Recovering a Sense of the Sacred.* What philosophy was being promoted? Was it an approach in which I could be active? Was it an approach in which I could believe and adopt? Actually, it was even more than that; it was a life lesson for making a shift in my life with the added effect of changing the world. Carolyn and Thomas were calling us to reconnect with the earth, to reconnect with nature. I was being asked to embrace my roots. I was being directed to fully embrace our universe by taking the time to appreciate its gifts and to protect them and to reach out and share this approach with anyone and everyone within my life's circle. So, here I am sharing this philosophy, maybe even better described as a theology, with all the people who read these missives.

Once again my lesson was coming to me in many different forms. The first was Carolyn's lecture; then I read her delightful, insightful book, and within the same week, I had the opportunity to visit the Conservatory in Washington, DC and marvel at the variety of plants our earth provides. The Conservatory takes you from the early 1800s, when plants were first being collected, until today, and also from the mountain foliage to that of the jungle and tropics. The first plant we saw when we walked into the greenhouse was a cacao tree. It took my breath away. There were these huge yellow pods hanging off the side of the tree, ready to be harvested and turned into cacao butter and chocolate. Each turn took us to another miracle: banana trees, fruit trees, ferns and cacti, lovely succulents and gorgeous orchids, every kind of tree and plant imaginable. I was more aware of the gifts in front of us because of the lecture I had recently attended.

I'm not much of a gardener. I'm not very good at tending houseplants. I have had gardens over the years, mostly vegetables, but I'm a city girl raised on a very busy highway with about eight square feet of lawn in front of our house and a small strip of dirt in the back for the dog to relieve himself. We never grew anything. We tried planting watermelon seeds one spring, but other than a massive vine, we didn't get any fruit. As an adult, as the care of the inside of our homes became more demanding, I spent less and less time outside in the dirt. Now, I was being called to reconnect with the earth.

After Carolyn led us in a guided meditation, she asked us what we believed we could do to make a difference. I had a very clear message: "Jean Anne, go outside." I have begun to work out a way to start and to nurture that process. Why? What is the message Carolyn is relaying from Thomas?

The only way to save the earth and humankind is to embrace nature. We are being called not to simply see our world as a place to meet our needs but as a place for which we are responsible and which needs our care and nurturing. It is time for me to recognize that unless we embrace our universe and all its majesty and miracles, it will not continue to thrive. If it is depleted and not appreciated, our existence will be compromised, if we are not made extinct. Thomas Berry declared, "As we practice a presence to the natural world through our intuition we come to know ourselves, not simply as physical beings, but as spiritual beings. We humans are modes of the Divine presence who have forgotten our identity with creation. We are one earth community that lives or dies together. We depend on the earth to sustain us in body and soul. We come into *relationship* to it instead of establishing an identity over and against it."

The rest of this week's lesson came when we entered the Native American Museum in DC. We began our tour on the fourth floor, where several of the larger tribes had been invited to display their heritage. There were stories about their costumes, their dances and songs, and especially about their reverence for Mother Earth: for the plants, the animals, the stars, and the wind. They honored all four of our elements: water, fire, wind, and earth. They not only experienced nature, they treasured it. They didn't just consume it. Even more important is that their major concern is teaching these lessons to the next generation and letting them know that they are responsible for all their future generations. "How will this decision affect my seventh generation?" was and is one of their key lessons.

My awareness of God's miracles seen in nature and my responsibility to honor and treasure those gifts have already begun to blossom. I am determined to "go outside" more often and to meditate on the stars as well as the weeds. I will tenderly hold a flower or attentively listen to the bird's song. I may not be able to care for the whole planet, but I am more than capable of caring for my small piece of it here in North Carolina. And perhaps by heightening my awareness, my tiny steps will make a difference in our universe. I believe that my efforts will have the added gift of not just appreciating our earth, but will lead me to a greater appreciation, perhaps a greater connection to the Divine and to my God. By learning to treasure the earth, I'll be able to have hope that my seventh generation will not only still be here on this planet and not off living on Mars or a satellite, but thriving right here on this amazing planet Earth.

10. Aging with Optimism

Affirmation: *The best is yet to come.*

On a delightful day in the North Carolina mountains, my friend Travis Tracy and I headed to the Boone Farmer's Market. What would we find? We found fresh-from-the-farm fruits and veggies, handcrafted pottery and jewelry, homemade jams and soaps, wild flowers and giant sunflowers, and a street musician or two. There were gifts for all of the senses and there were all types of people, from the farmers and craft people to the tourists and the "snowbirds." However, while we found loads of goodies, the neatest part of our outing was meeting a couple of the vendors who were not selling produce but services.

One young woman was there representing the Women's Sustainable Agriculture Association. The following Saturday was to be the local garden and farm tour. You would receive a map and for $15 you could spend the day driving from farm to farm. She was with AmeriCorps. She explained it was like the Peace Corps. Her two-year assignment was almost up, and when I asked her about her experience, she exclaimed that it was "Wonderful!" Wonderful! Wow, I immediately wanted to be in my early twenties and a volunteer, or perhaps I could at least share the concept with my grandchildren and encourage them toward "Wonderful."

Then we headed to the Daniel Boone Gardens, where they were sponsoring "Fairy Day." There were dozens of little girls skipping around in tutus, flowery headbands, and gossamer wings. Once again I wished I were younger and had a pair of those shiny, sparkly wings. Part of the event included a group from Appalachian State University. They were there representing the AgeLabs of the Psychology Department. The young woman, Lisa Emery, we stopped to chat with was a professor in that department, and they were looking for older adults to volunteer for some of their research projects. Would we be interested? Maybe.

As we talked we gravitated toward my favorite subject, our self-talk; how we create it and how it influences every aspect of our lives. She shared that one of the studies regarding aging and attitude showed a direct relationship between our later years and our perception of aging. For example, if one believes that one's memory will definitely deteriorate as one ages, one's memory will most likely become worse. What that preconceived notion also creates is a vacuum for a helpful medical diagnosis like a hormonal issue, a thyroid condition, or even perhaps a brain tumor. This belief system may lead to an earlier deterioration or even an early death.

What are your preconceived beliefs about aging? Do you think you must get heavier, weaker, less agile, more grumpy? Perhaps you think you'll be a worse driver, have no real purpose, or not find meaning in life anymore. Maybe you're someone who chooses to see the later years as a time of freedom and adventure. Guess what? The future you imagine is more likely to happen than not. Certainly, if you do not see a future filled with blessings and possibilities, even when they arrive you probably won't recognize them.

Sister Joan Chittister, in *The Gift of Years: Growing Older Gracefully*, says one of the challenges of aging is that there's no defined purpose to life after the age of seventy. Before that most people (not in a third-world country) are getting an education, then raising a family and developing a career, finally crafting a retirement plan and then *wham*! If you're one of the lucky ones, you're on your own to figure out what life without a societal definition looks like. I find Sister Chittister's writing to be uplifting and filled with hope. Her chapter on *Immediacy* reminded me, once again, of the power I have to choose moment to moment, day to day, on what I want to focus. She writes, "What we too often fail to realize is that living fully depends a great deal more on our frame of mind, our fundamental spirituality, than it does on our physical condition."

I find myself asking: How do I want to live out the years I have left? What words do I want to choose to craft a joyful, meaningful later life? I have some of the most inspirational older men and women in my life. I want to emulate them. I have one dear friend, Joanne Dawe, who at the time of this missive was almost retired and had prepared for it by taking up gardening at the NC Museum of Art, helping different chefs demonstrate their cooking techniques at a local kitchen shop, refurbishing furniture for people with limited incomes who are trying to set up a home, and also became a qualified barbecue judge. Another of my dear friends, Jean Scholz, is a phenomenal artist who founded and supported The Cary Gallery of Artists (co-op). Two of my heroines are Sisters Mary Margaret Weber and Judy Hallock, co-directors of A Place for Women to Gather in Raleigh, NC. At the Duke Cancer Patient Support Program, there are dozens of retirees who show up once a week and sometimes more often to be patient navigators and supporters. The list is endless of people who created meaningful, fulfilling lives after their years of defined work.

Some of my passions are learning, yoga, the fiddle, and writing. I love to travel too. I love a car trip. I actually took up the fiddle because of my deceased Uncle Frank. I never heard him play, but I knew he played with the Long Island Senior Symphony until his late nineties. He and my dearly departed Aunt Alice had a very rich older life revolving around their music and their church. I recognized that I might need something I could do while sitting. Little did I realize the physical toll violin playing or fiddling can take on the body. (I'm often asked, "What's the difference between a violin and a fiddle?" The answer came from a seven-year-old one day. "A violin has strings and a fiddle has strangs." It has been a joy learning how to fiddle. As an adult learner I still struggle, but I love, love, love playing.

I plan to stay strong. I see myself as still agile and alert. I see myself still trying new things and embracing new people and new ideas. I see myself surrounded by love and compassion. I see myself as still contributing any way possible, especially with prayer, to hopefully make this world a better place. I can't help but see some of the challenges and losses I will also face, but I see myself dealing with those the same way I've dealt with the ones in the past—with grace, dignity, and even some humor. I think the affirmation that most fits this concept of looking toward the future with excitement and optimism is: *The best is yet to come*. I can own those words. I can believe that with all the tools I've collected over my lifetime, especially that of my faith, family, and friends, life will be better as I age than it has ever been before.

11. Have Courage and Be Kind

Affirmation: *I live a Christ-centered life of love, hope, peace, gratitude, and compassion.*

Louise Penny, the author of the crime novels about Three Pines, Canada, and Inspector Gamache, came to Meredith College in September 2015 to promote her newest book, *The Nature of the Beast*. It's her twelfth book in this series. The auditorium was full. I guessed there were about three hundred people there. I became a fan a few years back when one of the women in my book group, Anne Brill, recommended Mrs. Penny's work. My husband, Sandy, and I like to listen to a good book if we have an extended drive, and I purchased *The Beautiful Mystery* for us. We were immediately hooked. We usually can't wait for our next long trip to delve into the newest novel and to be reunited with the Inspector and the rest of our new "friends."

Louise didn't really speak about her books because she said she might give away some of the storyline, which would interfere with her readers' enjoyment. Instead she spoke about her journey to becoming a successful writer. It wasn't an unusual story. It took her a long time and required quite a bit of stamina and also a few serendipitous events. One event revolved around a fund-raiser in a foreign country where she met her publisher, the only person with whom she had an encounter during the whole night. Her whole story was interesting but the message with which I came away was about kindness.

Louise said she modeled the inspector after her husband. If you've read any of her work, you will know the inspector is a wonderful man. He is a family man, he cares deeply about his coworkers, and he rises above the call of duty to a place of kindness and compassion. What a gift to have someone in your life like that, anyone, but especially the person with whom you've chosen to spend your life. I know it's a gift because I, too, have a husband like that. When she spoke about the qualities these men exemplify, she focused on kindness. It was a short sentence but it emphasized to me the power of words. "It is easier to be mean than it is to be kind." *Well*, I thought, *isn't that the truth!*

Don't you love it when the same message repeats itself in your life? Why, I wondered, was I hearing this concept on a regular basis? What was God or simply the Universe trying to tell me? What more am I to learn? I kept hearing the phrase "Have courage and be kind." I bet you didn't know that those were Cinderella's mother's last words to Ella. Disney's 2015 adaptation of the famous fairy tale added that phrase. In this edition, Cinderella wasn't simply saved by the handsome prince; the filmmakers chose to empower her with qualities that enabled her to change her life and still be compassionate. Thank heavens!

It seems to me it's so much easier for people to be spiteful, to be right, to be "all about me and not about you." We all recognize when we are being treated kindly. Are we called to be kind to everyone? It seems we are. We are even called to be kind to our enemies. What does that look like? Does it take more energy to be kind than mean or indifferent? Maybe it just takes a different kind of energy. I believe it certainly takes a more conscientious effort to rise to the higher good than to sink to the lowest common denominator.

Kindness is a close relative of compassion. Many of the messages I've received lately in several of my readings have revolved around my responsibility to show compassion for the marginalized and suffering of the world. Compassion is kindness put into action. I believe as I age that responsibility becomes even greater. This is a time in my life when I have the luxury of having more time, and how I use that time is very important. I want to leave this world a better place than I found it. I must confess there are many days when I look around and can't even imagine what steps I can take to help the world. It helps to recognize that I support several projects that reach beyond my normal sphere of influence to the benefit of those who need exceptional help. I can't help the whole world, but I can do some things that make a difference, or can I?

Do you know the story about the boy who is throwing starfish into the ocean? A man comes along and asks him what he's doing and the boy explains he's saving lives. The man laughs and tells him he's wasting his time; he can't possibly save all the starfish. It's not making a difference. The boy picks up another starfish and throws it into the ocean and says, "Well, I made a difference to that one." My sister, Gloria Hafner, was a specialized reading teacher in New York. She took one or two students at a time and helped them learn to read at or above age level. She always told anyone who would listen about her work that she had "made a difference to that one."

At the time of this entry, Pope Francis was about to come to the United States. There had been a lot of publicity around his visit. His approach to the world was causing quite a stir. He seemed to me to be filled with love and compassion. He wanted us all to fill ourselves with these intentions and then to put them into action. He didn't want to hear excuses and he didn't want to be our judge or jury. He was encouraging everyone to hear the message of Jesus and to go forward to make the world a better place. I found his message and his example to be refreshing, inspirational, and challenging.

One of my efforts revolves around my belief in the power of prayer. I am trusting that my prayers seep out into the universe and relieves some of the pain and suffering of someone. It seems to me there is so much anguish. Perhaps the world was always like it is now and we simply see it more clearly because of the media, but what is taking place, especially at this time, with the refugees from Syria and Africa is beyond tragic.

One of the conversations I've had recently was about energy and our ability to influence it. The scientist I spoke with didn't believe there was such a thing, and that the only reason there was any sort of change was due to a placebo effect. I didn't feel qualified to argue with him, but I left feeling very sad. He didn't believe in mystery. He only believed in *mastery*. He only seemed to believe in what he could see and touch and prove. I am sure he is not alone, but I need *mystery*. I need to believe that there is more to this life than what I perceive.

I don't believe there will ever be any definite proof that our thoughts and prayers change the world, but I truly believe they do. I actually embrace the mystery and imagine one day when I am no longer physically part of this world, being shown how the time and effort I made to send help to others through prayer manifested itself. It'll be my Judgment Day. I'll see where I failed to rise to the level of a higher plane and where I truly made a difference because I cared and was willing to take the time and make an effort to pray.

Maybe that's why lately the words "courage" and "kind" are being put together. It may be harder to be kind and it is a very important quality to practice, but it takes courage to be compassionate. It takes the ability to suffer with another, and that is very hard. It's so much easier to turn off the TV or to turn away from the homeless and hungry. Pope Francis and now even Disney were calling all of us to step outside of our comfort zone and find a way to help those in need. Perhaps it will be with prayer. Perhaps it will be only to reach out to one person, someone for whom we can claim, "It made a difference to that one."

12. Hugging for Health

Affirmation: *I gather ten hugs a day.*

My mother was of English-Scottish descent and my father was an only child whose father was Swiss-German. I don't know if that's why we didn't do a lot of hugging, but we didn't. My husband's family is pure Italian. Some are from Naples and others are from Sicily; both his mother and his father's family immigrated from Italy. When Sandy took me to his house to meet his family, the front door flew open and his mother, Yolanda, all five feet of her, threw open her arms and hugged me with all her might. I was home. I think I had waited my whole young life to be embraced with such ardor. This was where I belonged.

I read many years ago that we are supposed to gather ten hugs a day. I know some people don't like being touched. I know it's not appropriate to go around hugging everyone, but oh, how I love to give and get a hug. I've found it fascinating that once you tell someone about the ten hug a day quota, or at least the people I see regularly, they are excited about sharing a hug. I have adopted Yolanda's warm greeting with almost everyone who comes to our home. I feel my hug says, "Welcome! I'm so glad you're here! Come in and share the warmth and safety of our home."

In most of the groups I belong to, we greet each other with a hug. Touch is an essential part of staying healthy. During World War II psychologists noted that orphaned infants who were not cuddled suffered stunted growth both physically and mentally and in some instances actually died. Now we have all sorts of programs that insure babies will be held and even massaged to promote their healthy development. We all need to be touched. Massage has been shown to be an amazing tool in the arsenal for staying healthy. The elderly need touch. When I did my MSW at Chapel Hill, NC, I focused on gerontology. One of the topics discussed was how as we age many people don't get enough affection. Therefore, whenever I visit an assisted living or an Alzheimer's unit, I make sure to hold hands or touch the residents' arms or shoulders. If they seem agreeable to a hug, I freely give one.

There are so many ways to greet people, and so much of it is determined by the culture in which we reside. Of course it's also determined by the relationship we have with a person. In most cases we greet a complete stranger with a nod, perhaps a smile or a handshake. I've been in European countries where I was kissed on both cheeks by someone I'd just met. When I was at Kripalu studying Yoga, we had one full day of silence. It was not the first time I'd been in a silent mode at a retreat, but this time the teacher instructed us to not even make eye contact. She explained that even that type of communication required energy, and the purpose of this exercise was to completely focus within. It was the first time I was so aware of how much effort I put into my casual contacts. I can remember walking the quad in college and making an effort to acknowledge everyone I passed who I knew or who even looked familiar. I still do that. My walks around Apex Lake here in North Carolina contain many nods, smiles, and greetings. It seems so natural to me. I am always perplexed by those who have on their earpieces and don't even look my way as they pass by, but I do not judge them. Perhaps this is their "silent retreat" time.

My husband, Sandy, believes the Italians invented hugging, but my daughter-in-law, Belen, is from Ecuador and they, too, are great huggers. She has taught us how to greet every family member. You get up from wherever you are, and you go to the person who has just arrived, and you give them a warm hug and maybe even a kiss. Her greetings say, "I love you. You are important in my life." It's been another gift she has brought to our family.

There are many different types of hugs. There is the one-arm hug; the *wrap your arms around someone and hold them tenderly* hug; the bear hug; the group hug; the spoon hug; and the heart-to-heart hug. If you rest your left cheek on the other's left cheek and shift your weight to the right, your heart will rest on top of theirs and you'll feel its rhythm.

How do you greet people? What comes naturally? Do you think you can learn to hug if it doesn't come naturally? Once I was with a friend in a department store and I went and asked a salesperson a question. The sales associate wore a name tag and I called her by name. My friend was shocked that I would use someone's name to whom I had never been introduced. I love a name tag. I make every effort to read a service person's tag and to call them by name. For me, it's another type of a hug, a verbal hug. It's the same message we each send when we greet someone warmly. "I care about you. You are important."

Ten hugs a day keeps the doctor away. One day I walked into the choir room at St. Michael the Archangel to sing for a funeral. At this time I was with the Resurrection Choir. Wayne Cushner was the gifted music minister for all of our services. The room was packed with people because our former pastor was being buried, and the regular choir from two churches were singing. I was immediately embraced by several people. I found myself counting, *One, two, three, four, five.* Five hugs plus Sandy's early morning hug. *Six. Only four more to go,* I thought. *This will be an easy goal today.* Ten hugs a day keeps us healthy and keeps those healthy with whom we share them. A simple heartfelt hug can brighten your life and the lives of those you care about. Can you gather ten hugs today? Be careful, it's a random act of sharing joy and affection. Once you begin you might have to hold back with that stranger walking past you.

13. Blessed Are the Balanced

Affirmation: *I am fully aware of the importance of maintaining a healthy balance.*

Balance is another gift of yoga. There are the obvious asanas that offer the yogi the opportunity to practice balancing: headstand, dancer's pose, warrior III, and the classic tree pose to name a few, but unless you are lying on your back or stomach, balance is always involved in a pose, just like in life. We then have the opportunity of taking our balancing practice with us out into our day and into our world. What does it mean to balance? Is one ever balanced or is there only the practice of balancing?

At the time of this writing, I had taken on caring for a loved one. The care required much more effort than was required or desired in the past. I spent a great deal of time at the hospital, the rehab, and on the phone or on email connecting with caretakers, family, and friends. I was happy to do it. I loved her and was pleased to have the opportunity to do whatever was necessary to be of service, but life was extremely full. I now had the additional activities required for this caretaking and my normal full life.

When I was guided to do tree pose in a yoga class, I immediately placed all my weight on my right foot, the sole of my left foot against my inner thigh, and chose one spot on which to focus. I then put my hands over my head and became a tree. I had done this hundreds, maybe thousands of times. I was then guided to switch sides. I couldn't do it. My left leg would not hold my weight on its own. I needed help. I went to the wall in order to maintain my balance. I was stunned that the imbalance in my daily life was so glaringly presented to me in my pose. I didn't feel too worried about it because I recognized that while I was out of balance at the moment, I was now fully aware of it and I needed to attend to whatever it took to help me level out.

There are all kinds of balance: work and play, self-care and community service, calories in versus calories out, time alone and time with others, spending and saving money, exercise and rest. The list can go on and on. I'm sure you can think of a few, perhaps some on which you've been working. One challenging part of achieving balance is it's so personal. What is good for one person may not be true for another. Like any life skill one is trying to improve, the very first step is awareness, actually recognizing when you're out of sync. Another factor is the time frame it's placed within. Are we looking to be in balance every moment, every day, once a week, or are we content to look over the whole year and think something like, *I worked hard for most of the year and now I'm going to take it easy for the end of the year?*

The truth is balance is no different from dieting. First we need a focus point, perhaps a specific weight we are trying to maintain. Every day we make choices, and each choice will lead to a better balanced life. When you are watching calories, you can have a heavier day one day and a lighter one the next day to balance out your intake, or perhaps you are fairly conscientious during the week and that allows you to eat a little heavier on the weekend. If we take it one step further, perhaps you're fairly restrictive most of the year but let yourself relax while you're on vacation or at a celebration. As long as you can maintain your healthy weight, it doesn't matter how you do it; but you're going to have to balance out those calories or your weight will either climb or get too low. It's no different with anything else to which you want to bring balance.

Many years ago a very spiritual woman told me a story about her volunteer work. She was determined to become more faithful, and with that she decided to spend more time at her church, and then that became even more time. Finally, she was at the church all the time, and her family and her work were falling apart. She couldn't figure out what was wrong, if anything, because she was sure she was following the better path to God. Before her world came crashing down upon her, the parish priest counseled her to look at the imbalance of her life. She examined her priorities, made several changes, and saved herself. The path to holiness requires that we attend not just to the spirit but to the mind and to the body. That means the path to holiness requires balance or at least an ongoing attempt at balancing.

In order to walk the tightrope of life, we must be vigilant and place one foot gingerly and mindfully in front of the other. It takes practice.

It takes the lessons from the yoga mat and from wherever and whomever we can learn them. Perhaps with enough practice one will even be able to stand on one's head. If not, perhaps at least on one foot at a time, or even just both feet without toppling over.

The following week I took some extra "me" time, and when I returned to class, I once again was able to become a tree—on the right side and on the left side.

FALL

1. Owning Only My Own Behavior

Affirmation: *I am only responsible for my own behavior.*

In 2000 my husband and I attended a workshop at Canyon Ranch called *Sex, Body and Soul.* It was the year after I was treated for breast cancer and I asked him to go with me. I had been there several months earlier and heard Dr. Lana Holstein speak and decided it would be a good thing for us in which to participate. We'd been married more than twenty years by then, and it seemed to me we could use a little more knowledge other than what we'd brought to the relationship when we were in our early twenties. Sandy is a kind and gracious man, and he has spent most of our married life doing his best to make sure I'm happy. I am a lucky woman and I know it. In the case of accepting this invitation, it took a lot of courage and humility to go along with me, and I was very grateful when he accepted. Dr. Holstein and her husband, Dr. David Taylor, led the group and set up some ground rules right away. I never felt uncomfortable. Yes, we learned a great deal, but as with many learning experiences, the most important lesson had very little to do with the curriculum.

It was obvious from the beginning that one of the couples—there were about fifteen in attendance—was a strange match. She was all bubbly and floaty, and he was just plain grumpy. He did not want to be there and he told us right away, but he said he was there because he loved her and this was what she wanted to do. We were there for four days, and he complained the entire time. Watching her was my greatest learning experience at the workshop. She never paid any attention to his moaning. She just let him be himself and did whatever she wanted to do. She never grimaced or cringed when he would speak. She never, ever apologized for his behavior. After a short time, it was obvious she didn't hold herself responsible for his behavior, and because of her detachment, no one in the group held her responsible for his behavior. For me, it was pure enlightenment.

I'd like to tell you that after that experience I never again acted embarrassed because someone I was with acted inappropriately or in a way I felt reflected poor judgment. While I can grasp this lesson mentally, it will probably take me a lifetime to absorb it emotionally.

In the Al-Anon book *One Day at a Time,* one of the readings tells a story about a woman who had just begun the program and after a short time decided the best way to deal with her alcoholic husband was to ignore him. Up until that time, she would find him after falling out of bed, asleep on the floor. She'd help him up, put him back in bed, and then cover him up. Then she'd go to bed. After a couple of Al-Anon meetings, she decided she needed to take better care of herself. So, she decided she wouldn't help him. She'd leave him on the floor, step over him, and just go to bed. She shared this at one of the meetings. Members explained that wasn't exactly what the program promoted. She then came up with a happy medium. She decided to cover him with a blanket and then step over him and go to bed.

One time my husband and I found ourselves having dinner with a couple we had just met. As the dinner progressed, the fellow kept ordering drinks. By the end of the dinner, it was quite obvious that he was very drunk. I kept waiting for his wife to try and stop him from ordering. When that didn't happen, I began to wait for her to correct him. When that didn't happen, I thought maybe she'd get him away from the dinner and take him home. When that didn't happen, I thought she'd begin to look embarrassed. You guessed it. She never responded in any way. Once again, I saw myself completely absolve her of her husband's behavior. She simply allowed him to be responsible for himself. She was sober and elegant and classy, and I was in awe.

I had a friend tell me once that if her husband ever fell asleep in church, she would be furious. I wondered why? Maybe he snored. Would his being asleep embarrass her? Why should it? She would still be awake. Would someone look over, or the preacher look out and see him sleeping and say, "Look at that woman next to the sleeping man. I bet that's his wife. She must be a terrible person to allow him to sleep during the service." If someone is judging you because of your companion's behavior, is that someone you care about? Is that someone who you even want to know?

I wonder if we learn this kind of reaction from being a parent. I think most people would agree that a parent is judged by their children's behavior. How many times have you been in a situation when a child behaved poorly and you just wanted the parent to "do something" to correct the problem? In Stephen Covey's book *The 7 Habits of Highly Effective People,* he tells the story of a man on the subway with a couple of poorly behaved children. People were obviously annoyed. Finally, the father looked up and said, "My wife just died and I don't know what I should be doing." People were no longer annoyed, but why did he have to share that? Why were people judging in the first place? Why, if they were, didn't they give him the benefit of the doubt?

Is this a control issue? Do we feel we should be able to shape the atmosphere and therefore influence the behavior of those to whom we are close? Once we recognize that we can't change anyone else, we can only change ourselves, perhaps then we can learn to just let go and let people be whomever they are, even if they're complete jerks.

Another story in the *One Day at a Time* Al-Anon book refers to a tombstone that reads, "Here lies Morty Mort. He's finally minding his own business." I hope by the time I'm laid to rest, I have finally absorbed the lesson that ***I am only responsible for my own behavior*** into not only my mind, but my heart and my spirit.

2. The Demise of Cursive Writing

Affirmation: *I am a lifelong learner.*

The conversation with my children was about writing. It wasn't about creative writing; it was about penmanship. Well, there's an old-fashioned word. I didn't know how outdated it was until we had this discussion. I was informed by my adult daughter, Melissa, that cursive writing sometime around the year of 2015 was no longer part of the core curriculum in the North Carolina school system. After the third grade, children are not taught how to write longhand. I'm still in shock. I've been writing three pages of longhand in my journal every morning for over fifteen years. My adult son, Joey, went on to say that he almost never uses a pen or a pencil. When he does, he finds them awkward to use. His writing method is almost always a keyboard. Penmanship is no longer considered an essential life skill.

That certainly wasn't true when I was in school. The cursive alphabet was on long strips of black paper resting above the blackboard. Yes, the board was black, not white, and we used chalk, not erasable Magic Markers. There were several lines on the paper, and each one was a height that determined where a loop, a "t," an "i," or a capital letter was to land on the page. We were handed blank lined pages, and we tried to copy the letters onto the paper from the form above the boards. We used number two pencils with erasers. I loved it! I liked the form and the lines for guidance and the feel of the pencil on the paper, and I loved seeing the letters take shape and appear on the page. I became a math teacher later in life. I was never much for coloring outside the lines, so it seems fairly understandable why I liked the rigid format that was used to learn cursive.

I've always been fascinated by handwriting. Some is legible and others completely illegible. Some is neat and clean and others are sloppy. Some is flowery and others are straight up and down. People have made a living "reading" handwriting. They are supposed to be able to figure out a person's personality from what their handwriting looks like. Not anymore! Did you ever watch a detective show where the sleuth looked at a typewritten note and determined whether someone was right-handed or left-handed because of how some of the letters appeared darker? They had been hit harder by the dominant hand. Not anymore! I went to summer school to learn how to type. My mother told me it was an invaluable life skill. She was right! The keyboard I use today is laid out exactly the same as the one that was on my manual typewriter. If you don't know what a typewriter looks like, Google it. But they don't teach typing in school anymore either. I think it comes already hard-wired in the brains of anyone born after 1990. I've seen two-year-olds working a computer keyboard.

Reading, writing, and arithmetic were the three "Rs" that we were told were the core skills we would need for life. The question about why we needed to learn mathematics when most people would never use it once they were out of school is decades old. As a math teacher, I sometimes wondered the same thing, but I knew the value of making the brain work in different ways, and for me there was always a great satisfaction in solving a problem correctly. I loved solving the "puzzle." But it's true, most people didn't have any use for algebra or geometry or trigonometry once they finished with the class. Now, most people don't even need to know the basics of math. There's a calculator on every phone. It appears to be one more life skill we no longer need.

So, that leaves reading as the last core skill we were told we needed. I can't imagine not reading. I love a good book. Recently I had cataract surgery, and the lenses that were implanted were determined by whether or not I read books and papers regularly or if I read from a computer. Can you imagine not being able to read? There are organizations dedicated to teaching adults how to read. It seems it still is an essential life skill. I wonder, however, will that always be true? Recently, I downloaded an app called OverDrive. It allows me to connect to my library and to download audio books onto my phone or iPad. I can then listen to the book wherever and whenever I want. I know there have been audio books for decades, but now they are prolific and free; for many it's their preferred way to "read" a book. What does this foretell?

If we don't need to learn the three "Rs" any longer, what do we need to learn, or even more important, what do we need to be teaching? What are the schools focusing on that is preparing our young people to live meaningful, productive lives? We have several people in the family who have been diagnosed with attention deficit disorder (ADD). I know it is more commonly diagnosed today than ever before. I'm not sure if it's because more people struggle with it or because we're more knowledgeable about it. At one point one of my grandsons was really struggling in his traditional middle school because of ADD. We were fortunate to find a small local school that had a different, more hands-on approach to learning. Once there he blossomed both mentally and emotionally. His learning "style" needed a place with a different environment in order for it to take root. What was he learning at his new school that was different from the other one? He learned how to learn.

Let's face it, all the information we need or want to learn about is available to us in one form or another. Today it's even more readily available because of our access to the Internet. I am in awe of the range of information available online. There are lessons on everything! There are lessons about things I probably don't want to know anything about. I have, however, looked up music lessons and how to fix different things. My son uses the Internet to renovate equipment like boats, cars, engines, and all sorts of electronic equipment. The other day our refrigerator broke down, and the first thing we did, after throwing away the perishables, was to go online to see if we could diagnose it and fix it ourselves. Owen, my youngest grandson, is always telling me about different places he's never been to or about scientific data he's looked up. It's beyond exciting! Back in March of 2013, Owen pretended to be a reporter and interviewed Galileo about his theories. My husband, Sandy, played the role of the famous scientist. It was for Owen's science project. Everyone learned something and it was fun.

I'd like to think that our educational system is closely examining what our young people need to learn in order to be productive, healthy citizens. What do you think the new core skills should be? It seems to me one of the most important ones would be to learn how to learn. Owen is an experiential learner. Once he discovered that, he found he could learn whatever he wanted. I am mainly an auditory learner. If I had known that earlier on, learning would have come a lot easier to me. Some of us are visual; others need a variety of approaches. Once we've learned how to gather the information, the rest is just doing it. But what other core skills do we want our children to master? What are the essential life skills? If it's true we learn all we need to know in kindergarten, what are we doing with the rest of our years of schooling? How about focusing on the Golden Rule? "Do unto others as you would have them do unto you." How about the Ten Commandments? What about relationship skills: how to resolve conflict, how to create community, how to get your needs met without hurting another? What if the three "Rs" morphed into the three "Cs": compassion, communication, and cooperation?

Yes, we still need to know how to read and write; if not in cursive, then at least we need to know how to compose a grammatically correct sentence. The key, however, to all of this is it's not so much what we learn but that we do learn and not just while we're in school but for as long as we're alive. Expand your knowledge. Go out there and learn about life, learn about living, learn whatever it is that makes you feel fully alive. Then perhaps you'll write about it. Perhaps you'll share it with the world. Who knows, maybe someday someone will download and listen to it.

3. Just Pick Up the Phone

Affirmation: *When I quickly and directly resolve an issue, I feel less stressed and more peaceful.*

At the time of this entry, the age of electronic communications has dawned and blossomed. On *Longmire*, one of my favorite TV shows, Longmire's deputy checked the victim's phone for text messages rather than for phone calls. And that was the correct method for finding out about the victim's activity. It's so easy to send a text, an email, or a tweet, but it isn't necessarily the quickest way to communicate with someone. One day my grandson texted me from another room in our home to ask me a question. I thought he'd left without telling me and I panicked, but he hadn't. He was thirteen at this time; he was lucky he made it to fourteen.

Once, I had several situations that were making me a little anxious. In all cases I had emailed the person or the company and had either not received an answer or I didn't get the answer I wanted. The first issue was with amazon.com. I had bought a faucet for our kitchen. The kitchen was being remodeled, and by the time the plumbers were ready to install the faucet, my return date had passed. The faucet didn't fit. When I went online to return it, I got the pop-up that it was too late to send it back. I was quite annoyed and then I thought, *Just pick up the phone*. I had a quick conversation with a very nice person who waived the return date so I could send it back. It was easy but if I hadn't made the phone call, I'd still own that faucet.

I was on a roll now. I'd become my mom's financial caretaker. She had always done an amazing job with her resources, but it had become too much for her. Her credit card bill came and I put it on the shelf. For the first time in her life, her next credit card bill came with a service charge on it. Oh my! I was in trouble! It was quite a penalty for a very small overdue balance. I picked up the phone and spoke with a very nice young woman. I guessed she could immediately see the bill had never been late before and she immediately took off the penalty fee. Whew!

It seems this was the lesson I needed to learn at that time. Once I began looking at different situations with an eye toward finding easier, quicker resolutions, more and more opportunities kept presenting themselves. I found with each episode that came up, if I acted immediately and directly rather than just mulling over what to do, I was less stressed and more peaceful.

The faucet wasn't the only remodeling snafu. We had hired a very nice young man to be our contractor, and he seemed quite efficient. At the beginning of the project, he put together some sort of computer notification system that showed us the exact time required for each part of the job and the exact cost of every single step. Over the next few weeks, that program would pop up almost daily with some sort of time change or, even worse, *price* increase. Needless to say I was becoming more and more anxious every time I'd see an email with his company's name on it. At first I found my stomach would knot up and my head would begin to ache, but then I changed my approach. When something was changed, I'd call him and many times he'd relieve my anxiety with a detailed explanation, or he'd remove the extra fee because he'd made a mistake. (I chose to believe it was an error.) With that phone call came the ability for me to take deeper breaths and relax about whatever was being presented.

Even with my family I've noticed how often we now text or email one another rather than calling, although not as readily as my grandson. All too often I wasn't getting an answer to my questions or they were wondering why I hadn't replied to their queries. Usually it was because the emails got lost in the ether somewhere. But with a simple phone call, whatever question we had would be resolved, immediately.

Since this was my lesson for now, I began to wonder if I shouldn't apply it to my prayer life too. How often did I obsess over some life issue that needed to be let go of and turned over to God? What if I took my new lesson and, rather than letting the issue weigh me down, I immediately "picked up the phone" and shared it with the Lord? What would that look like? What number would I dial? I closed my eyes and sat quietly and envisioned the phone. It wasn't a cell phone. Interestingly, it was an old-fashioned phone like the one in *Dr. Strangelove* with Peter Sellers and it was red. I guess it was because in the movie the red phone was a direct line to the President. I didn't need a phone number at all. I just needed to pick up that old-fashioned red phone and God would be on the other end. God is always on the other end, waiting for me to call. Once I've taken the time and made the effort to connect, I am connected. No, the situation may not be resolved as quickly as it was at amazon.com or L.L.Bean, although it might be, but I quickly realized I felt better about my concerns. By taking the time to "call" God, I felt less stressed and I felt more peaceful.

4. Un-attaching

Affirmation: *I love unconditionally, nonjudgmentally, and without attachment.*

When my husband and I went to the Grand Canyon, we took a walk along the south ridge, and there in the middle of the walk was a logged bench. It must have weighed a couple of tons. It was a lovely spot over which to look out. When we rose, we noticed that the bench had been chained down. What we couldn't figure out was why. It seemed virtually impossible for someone to move the bench, no less pick it up and take it away. I can only guess they had their reasons. Maybe they needed to give someone a job and they made that one up. Maybe they caught a few people trying to move the bench and decided not to take any chances. Maybe you can think up a couple of reasons why they felt they needed to chain down a bench of that size and weight.

Over 2,000 years ago Patanjali, the grandfather of Yoga, recorded Yoga sutras (threads of wisdom) that can help us cope with limitations of the human condition. In writings that reflected the knowledge of all the yogis before him, Patanjali claimed that these practices would help conquer the five human afflictions that cause suffering (kleshas): ignorance, egoism, aversion, possessiveness, and attachment.

I have read that in India loggers use elephants to help them do their work. They begin training the elephants from the time they are very young. One of the training tools is a stake and a chain. They chain a baby elephant to a stake so it will stay put. When the elephant is an adult, they use the same procedure. The adult elephant still stays where it is put because it believes it cannot free itself.

In both cases, with the bench and with the elephant the chains are superfluous. They serve no purpose whatsoever. They are simply used to give the illusion that the item needs to be attached to something.

It is the season of Advent as I write this. We have been inundated with advertisements about all the stuff we should want—want for ourselves and want for others. And along with all the material possessions by which we are seduced, there is also the expectations we have about what the holidays will be like, whom we will be with, what events will take place, how much attention we will receive or are expected to give. We are attached to so many things, material and emotional. These can be the chains we have created that keep us connected to things we don't really need to be connected to; chains that we've created that are useless, superfluous. Can you see why Patanjali thought attachment was a human affliction?

One of my affirmations is*: I love unconditionally, nonjudgmentally, and without attachment.* It means I must leave my ego and my expectations aside. Of course, being human means we do become attached to people and things, but not feeling like you own them and they are fully yours takes effort.

Have you ever had the pleasure of watching the Tibetan monks create a sand mandala? When they came here to Raleigh to the North Carolina Museum of Art, I went to watch them create it. They had these little tiny tubes of colored sand and they placed the sand grain by grain where they wanted it in order to make the picture. I'd say it was about six feet square. It took about a week. I also attended the final ceremony. They scooped up all the sand and walked it to the lake and poured it in. They completely let it go; they released it.

I'm sure it's the same as the artists who do the sand sculptures or the ones who do the chalk drawings. I find it fascinating that someone can spend so much time creating something so remarkable and beautiful and yet know that it will not last, it will wash away. All mothers and fathers create this precious one-of-a-kind piece of art, our children. Perhaps that's the final lesson. All the things of this earth, of this world, of our world will not last; they will one day be gone. If we can find a way to embrace that concept, life will be less painful, more serene.

I have a vision that not only has the elephant finally found its freedom but so has that bench. Just like in the cartoons, it looks down, sees that silly chain, and snaps it off as it goes to find its perfect location; as it goes to find its freedom and its bliss. What do your chains look like? What attachments are causing you angst or sadness? How long have they been holding you there? What would it take for you to break the chain or to at least pull it out so you can run free?

5. Being a Victim

Affirmation: *I rest in the inquiry. I stand in my power.*

The young woman named Dina (one of our tour directors) was giving a description of Austria, and she was clever and quite funny. She came from Vienna, and because of that I felt very comfortable when she described a "typical" Austrian. "We are a people who always feel like we are being victimized. Tell me a tale about one of your problems and I will tell you one about myself that is worse than yours. We have a black cloud always hovering above us. The good news is we don't take ourselves too seriously, so we can laugh at our problems." I was fascinated. I wondered why the Austrian people had this impression about their lives. Was it nature or nurture? Certainly they had been through some terrible times. The tales we heard about the experiences of the people of Eastern Europe were beyond sad and extremely disturbing. I wondered if all the people in countries that had experienced horrible historical eras had the same general sense of being victims. What about Russia, Estonia, Slovakia, Hungary, Poland, North Korea, or Japan? How about Vietnam? What about the Mideast or some parts of Africa? Do the people in all of these areas of the world feel like victims?

I don't like to classify an entire population into one category, but certain characteristics do seem more prevalent in some cultures than in others. For instance, when my husband, Sandy, and I traveled through Ireland, we discovered the Irish people love to help lost travelers. They certainly loved helping us. We were always lost, and they couldn't do enough to get us back on the right road. We stopped to talk to one fellow out in the countryside who stopped mowing his lawn to give us directions and just about invited us in for tea. I'm sure if I named a nationality, you would come up with an adjective or two that you believe described them. How about the Italians, the Japanese, the Germans, or the Latinos? Did a couple of words pop up for you?

There have been times in my life when I could have felt like a victim. I remember people asking me if I wondered why I had developed breast cancer. Did I rail at God, "Why me, Lord?" No, I did not. It never occurred to me to even ask that question. Dr. Mark Graham told me it wasn't anything I did or did not do; it was a "random act of violence." That might have made me feel even more vulnerable, but for some reason it brought me a sense of peace. The thought came to me after listening to our guide that I probably don't have any Austrian blood in me. I couldn't imagine living a life where I always went around feeling victimized. How would that improve the quality of my life? I think I'd be a real grump and a very unhappy person. It certainly wouldn't fit in with my concept of creating an intentional life, a life of peace and love, joy, compassion, and gratitude. However, upon more careful consideration, I realized there have been many times in my life when I found myself feeling powerless, small, and insignificant. At those moments I did not step up and out. I did not claim my power, and even in the midst of "random acts," we still have choices. We still have the opportunity to decide how we perceive our situation and what we are going to do or not do.

I asked Dina, sometimes referred to as Dina Marie, and her coworker Scott, whose home was at that time in China, if in their travels they had noticed this victimization attitude in other countries where the people had experienced years of suffering and repression. They said they hadn't really thought about it. The documentary *The Singing Revolution* takes place in Estonia. It was an excellent film depicting life in Estonia through the last hundred years, and it presented a people who, even though they were suffering, decided to continue their ancient tradition of a mass singalong. It presented a picture of hope and positive behavior even during those most difficult of times. I've read and watched a lot of stories about WWI and WWII and about man's inhumanity toward man, especially about the horrors committed against the Jewish people. As we traveled through Eastern Europe and listened to the guides describe the situations which caused the deaths of so many people, thousands upon thousands, or through which they lived, I began to understand why the people in these countries would still feel a sense of travesty and powerlessness. To be completely honest, however, I know, with a capital "K," that I have never experienced the repression and torment that so many in the world have in the past or are presently experiencing. I probably cannot even imagine the horrors that are taking place. On our last evening of this trip, Scott, also affectionately known as Scotty Boy, left us all with this advice: "Now that you have traveled this part of the world, maybe the next time you see or hear of something distressing that they are experiencing, you will feel a deeper connection, a greater sense of compassion." He mentioned that one way to break down the barriers of prejudice and hatred is to be exposed to another's culture. I am hoping that faced with such struggle, I could muster enough strength—perhaps because of my relationship with my God—that I would not perceive my situation as hopeless.

The lesson here for me was that we always have a choice about how we want to perceive our situation. The more I thought about this feeling of being a victim, the more I realized it is not unusual for people to perceive themselves as victims even if they have never lived in a war-torn country. Most of the people I have known have lived in the US and are part of the blessed minority like myself who have not gone through the horrors of war and oppression. The people I've met who perceive themselves as victims are the people who believe that whatever happens to them is totally beyond their control; there is nothing they can do about it. They don't or can't recognize that even in the most dire of situations, we can choose to believe that we at some point can effect change. Our sense of purpose and power lies within us, not beyond our control. Daily we are called up to look at our attitudes and examine our beliefs and then to rise up and claim our power. If we practice daily in the smaller things of life, perhaps if and when we are faced with the larger, more daunting events, we will be able to "rest in the inquiry and stand in our power."

6. Claiming Courage

Affirmation: *I am courageous.*

"I learned that courage is not the absence of fear, but the triumph over it. The brave man is not the one who does not feel afraid, but he who conquers that fear." Nelson Mandela

It seemed to me the topic of many of my conversations often turned to the concept of courage. Partly because my Women of Grace study group was at this time reading *Ten Prayers God Always Says Yes To* by Anthony DeStefano. One of the prayers is "God, grant me courage." I loved the chapter on this topic. I thought his presentation was clear and comprehensive and just what I needed to "hear."

I know I have at least two positive affirmations that have bolstered my confidence over the years: *I am a bold adventuress and I am audacious* and *I say "Yes, I can."* They have worked quite well for me. Many times I've jumped into situations—well, okay, maybe I simply walked into them—that I was not sure about. I'd usually come out the other side excited about what had taken place and exhilarated that I'd overcome my fear and anxiety. It was usually a very empowering experience.

While those affirmations have been good, most of my days are fairly uneventful or at least not adventurous, and yet I can carry with me a sense of concern; concern about my finances, my health or that of my loved ones, my relationships, and especially about the future.

Part of Anthony's premise was that we need to practice being courageous. We need to pick up the quality, the gift every day. At first we should start with small things, and as our strength grows and our courage muscle becomes stronger, we will be able to be courageous at more challenging times. They are a coming! Or perhaps they are already here. The words were, for me, filling a need.

At this time I was still grieving the death of my mother and the blessed but very difficult last years of her life. I knew I would heal, but the memory lingered and weighed on me and left me wondering about my future, my old age, and my own death.

Think about the brave people you know. Think about the brave people you have read about. The first group that always comes to my mind are our service people. Some discovered courage in situations they never imagined they could endure. Our veterans are some of our most remarkable heroes. Then our firefighters come to mind. My dad, Frank Grolimund, was a captain with the New York City volunteer firefighters. I vividly remember being with him as he ran into a burning building to help with whatever was necessary. I believe he was very brave, if not a little crazy. I think, too, of all the firefighters who ran toward the dangers of the World Trade Center on 9/11. The memory still brings tears to my eyes. Then there's all those people fighting cancer or some other life-threatening illness. I am here to tell you, it takes an enormous amount of courage to continue that fight and, sometimes even more, to allow yourself or a loved one to let go.

The greatest example of courage for me, however, is that of Jesus Christ. When I meditate on His time in the Garden of Gethsemane (Matthew 26:36-46), I cannot imagine the courage it must have taken to give Himself completely over to His Father and get up and walk out to what He knew, in every excruciating detail, what He was to experience! He must have asked His Father for courage that evening, and it was obviously granted.

Now, I have learned that God will also grant me courage if I only ask. It will be one more answered prayer, and I don't have to wait. I can claim it now. I can claim it daily in all things, small and, with practice, large. "God, grant me courage," I am asking and I believe in answered prayer. With that comes a new affirmation: *I am courageous.*

How about you? Want to overcome fear and become brave? Want more courage? Join me. Ask!

7. Being Catholic

Affirmation: *I love being a Catholic.*

During October 2014, the Catholic Church was front-page news. It is not unusual for the Church to be in the headlines. It seems to me it's an easy target for criticism, especially in this day and time and sometimes for very valid reasons. This time, however, the initial news being reported was more positive. Pope Francis called a synod, a group of bishops from around the world, and the discussion that came from that meeting was highly publicized. It's unclear if everything that was written about the meeting was true, but that's nothing new for the media. The initial bent of the stories would lead most people to believe that the Catholic Church has decided to become more liberal.

At St. Benedict's Church in Linville, NC, Father Christopher Gober's homily revolved around the procedures that are required before the Church, or what I would prefer to refer to as the hierarchy, makes any changes in Church doctrine. "It will take years." Well, it doesn't take a genius to figure that out. The two-thousand-year-old church has never been quick to make any changes. It took them several hundred years to forgive Galileo, whom they excommunicated, because he claimed the earth revolved around the sun. With a mentality like that, those of us, including me, who are ever hopeful that our Church will become more open and accepting are not holding our breath. But there are some signs that our Church, the people who make up the foundation of our parishes, may see a shift toward compassion and inclusion that hasn't been focused on until this time in 2014.

Before the synod ever began, I was listening to a Tapestry podcast with Mary Hynes called "Liars, Cheats and Sinners," and the writer she was interviewing, described as a Roman Catholic thinker, Mary Gordon, said she didn't expect anything would be discussed that would make a difference for the laity. She, however, I am pleased to say, was wrong. Even if the doctrines are the same and it takes years, if ever, to make changes, Pope Francis seems to bring a whole different flavor to the meaning of our faith. When the leader of an institution calls for compassion and inclusion; when a leader in an institution is humble and deferential; and when a leader of an institution leads by example and not simply with words, the institution will reflect those qualities. And that, it seems to me, is Pope Francis.

I may be grasping at straws here, hoping that Pope Francis will bring our Church to a place where people don't usually feel as if they simply can't ever get it right; where people find it too difficult to be part of such a restrictive environment; where many people are forced to make decisions that are at conflict with the teachings of the Church simply to justify remaining in it. Why does it have to be so hard? I know in many ways the Catholic Church is a liberal institution if you compare it to many other fundamental faiths of the world, but in my opinion some of the stands it takes on issues that affect so many of its faithful are just wrong. My hope is Pope Francis will lead these men to a place of compassion and openness so that the fastest growing religion in the United States today is not "former Catholics."

Our Church has so much to offer, and because of all the bad publicity, some of which is justified, we aren't recognized for all our Church has done and continues to do to make this world a better place. For example, the Catholic Church feeds, educates, and tends to the health of tens of thousands of people a day. The people they serve aren't asked about their belief system or about their religion; they are simply helped. Why isn't that ever written about in the news?

I once had someone tell me she was an Episcopalian because, unlike Catholics, she didn't have to leave her brain at the church door. I can't even imagine why someone would think it was all right to say that to anyone, but trust me, that's not true. I have carefully considered whether or not I want to continue to be a Catholic. I've headed out many times; I've studied many faiths; I've read many different theologies. I finally had to recognize that I was always called back to Catholicism. Maybe, just by being who I am, I can make a difference in the way the Church responds to some of these controversial issues. Certainly, I have a better chance than if I walked away; if I simply quit.

I had one very powerful experience of asking God in prayer what path I should follow. I didn't know how the answer would come, but I believe in answered prayer and I did expect an answer. The answer came in a dream. Jesus floated down. He wasn't very clear, but I was pretty sure the white floating being was divine. He said, "Jean, I am the answer for you." I believed it then and I still believe it now. I have a dear friend who has told me for years, "I don't let the Church interfere with my relationship with God." That's not good enough for me. My Church needs practices and rituals that enhance and strengthen my relationship with God and, with that, my relationships with my family, my friends, and even my enemies.

I love the Catholic Church. I love being a Catholic. Yes, I know it has zits and dysfunction. What family doesn't? I have chosen to stay in this family, this place where the people with whom I interact are more often than not kind, generous, compassionate, and loving. I'm still a Catholic because of my belief in the sanctity of the Eucharist and the rituals of the mass and our seven sacraments.

The last headline I saw about the synod before I wrote this gave me hope. It said Pope Francis tells us: "God is not afraid of new things." Yes, I believe we are finally in the hands and heart of a loving, compassionate person who will bring our church to a place of more acceptance and kindness; who will help our parishes become places of refuge and hope; who will guide the hierarchy toward being less rule-oriented and more people-oriented. I'm not hopeful about changes in the perception of women's roles, but that's a whole other topic. I believe, however, that Pope Francis hasn't left his brain or his heart at the door, and I don't believe he expects us to live our faith and our lives without deep thought and commitment.

8. Blessings Recognized

Affirmation: *I recognize the blessings I receive when I share my time, treasure, and talent with those in need.*

On two occasions during October 2013, my husband, Sandy, was invited to be the Master of Ceremonies for the Ronald McDonald House of Durham, NC. The events began at 7:45 a.m. and lasted an hour. A full breakfast was served along with some of the most heart-warming and heart-wrenching stories I have ever heard. For me, the stories that reflect the struggle to live are always both inspirational and in many cases achingly sad. This event revolves around the challenges being faced by children, little tiny ones and their families, and the service, the hope and the comfort that this organization provides for them regardless of who they are or how much they have. The Ronald McDonald House had set up these two breakfasts, among other events, to give others the opportunity to be of service to their residents and future residents. They are giving people the opportunity to reach out and to make a difference in the life of someone who is suffering, someone they probably do not even know.

The first event of the month was at The Tobacco Warehouse in Durham, and about four hundred people attended. Sandy didn't say much to me about his role, and he's often invited to speak to groups, both large and small, so I didn't pay a lot of attention to his project. Sometimes he speaks for a fee, but many times he speaks to simply be of service. This, of course, was an example of the latter. I was pleased for him that he was asked and was given the opportunity, but I didn't attend. Actually, he didn't invite me and I wrote it off as simply another of his speaking engagements. Wow, did I get that one wrong!

He invited me to the second event, held in Raleigh at the NC State McKimmon Center. A friend and pet therapy volunteer, Ann Henderson, asked me to sit with her group of invitees. I was delighted to be included. Ann brought Bailey, her wonderful, warm, friendly doggie. The two of them also used to visit my mom once a week at my mom's assisted living apartment. It was the highlight of my mom"s week. So I can imagine how much joy Ann and Bailey bring to the residents of the Ronald McDonald House. They raised an amazing $260,000 during the one-hour breakfast. Why?

Sandy wasn't the only host. He had a co-host, Sosa. Sosa was thirteen. She wore a black dress with silver sequins across the top. She walked to that podium like she did it every day. I was once told the second greatest fear after death is speaking into a microphone. It was obvious Sosa had already conquered her first fear. She then started by apologizing for not wearing the red sneakers with the orange laces that she had been given, her Ronald McDonald sneakers. "They really don't go with my outfit," she said. Then she shared what it meant to her and her family to have a place, the Ronald McDonald House, to stay while she was receiving her second bone marrow transplant. Her mother had slept in their car for two months until space became available at "The House."

During the breakfast there were four other speakers: three sets of parents and Oie Osterkamp, the director of the Durham Ronald McDonald House. There was also a video which showed the journey of another teenage girl. I cried on and off throughout the entire program. Who wouldn't? Who can be among families who have undergone so much in an effort to make sure their child survives and not be emotionally moved? Obviously, not many of us. When Sandy finally made the plea for money, the audience responded with generosity and caring. The pledge card was not just for money. It also included a section for visits and volunteers. They accept any help they can get. I have friends who shop for, purchase, and cook one meal a month for the entire RMH in Greensboro, NC. Time, treasure, and talent are all greatly appreciated.

My experience has taught me that whenever I think I'm being magnanimous and generous to someone or to some cause, I discover that I am the receiver more than the giver. It's a gift to me when someone invites me into their lives and permits me to be of service. The book I had been reading, *Catching Fire, Becoming Flame*, said our first responsibility is to be of service to those who are less fortunate than we. Discovering what our gifts are and how we can best help another is actually a responsibility. We are called to service. We are called to help and support one another.

If you watch the news, we are led to believe we are not a caring species. The media almost never reports on something uplifting and positive. But Sandy and I have always been involved in many different charities, and we know people, both of our church and of no church, who lead lives which epitomize the phrase "giving back." It seems to me if we watch our fellow men and women carefully, we will see we are a caring, generous, even loving species. We like to help others. We like to make a positive difference in the lives of those around us, both those we know and in the case of these two breakfasts, in the lives of complete strangers. We must be an amazing group of beings.

These two one-hour events raised over $400,000, and I am sure they also generated a lot of interest for volunteer opportunities. Most people want to help others. Sometimes it simply takes being presented with an opportunity. These two events were a perfect example of creating an opportunity for people to feel good about themselves by sharing their bounty with others. For me, the blessing was to be included in my husband's caring spirit. Actually, one of my greatest blessings is that I am an integral part of Sandy's generous, loving heart.

9. Becoming Green

Affirmation: *I recognize my responsibility to be a good steward of Mother Earth.*

The retreat day topic presented by Sisters Mary Margaret and Judy from A Place for Women to Gather was "Oh Earth, I Cannot Hold You Close Enough." It revolved around a lovely painted image. The morning was devoted to quiet time and reflection time for us to attune to the beauty and bounty that the earth offers us with the final intention of finding ways we as individuals will support and care for our planet.

The *60 Minutes* segment presented on Sunday, November 16, 2014 was about our water consumption throughout the world. My home is Cary, North Carolina, and when I wrote this we already had had water restrictions for years, way before there was much of a visible issue and way before we even had any major problems with our water supply. Because of our town's efforts the water level for our area was healthy, but we hadn't always been "safe," and so our community had done an excellent job of encouraging people to conserve their water usage. They offered rebates for low-flow toilet and sold inexpensive rain barrels, and watering lawns and shrubs was restricted. The *60 Minutes* segment showed that small steps like our community took are more important than I had ever imagined, but they are not enough to keep our planet green and healthy. We are drilling for water like we do for oil, and we are sucking the earth dry.

The folks who monitor our water levels have for years used the primitive method of simply measuring the water table with a long tape measure lowered into holes throughout the world, and they have seen a huge decrease in the water table, more so over the last decade than ever before. Then a satellite was designed that takes photos of the whole world and whose sensitivity to moisture allows it to color the computer image based on how much water is present in the area. Green is healthy, red is sick, black is death. Over the last several years since about 2005, the computer images show that many of our world's major water tables have died. I know this is a simplistic explanation of a complex and serious issue. It did, however, cause me to be even more aware of which issues our beautiful planet is suffering from.

Once again I was faced with the question "What can I do to effect a change in this world, me, one tiny woman living in Cary, North Carolina?" My first thought was to pray. I was already praying for many worldwide issues, especially for those who are suffering the most. I know God knows who they are. I trusted She would hear my prayer and along with those of others, someone or even many would be comforted. On NPR during this time, the head of the UN's humanitarian services stated that there were now 59,000,000 displaced people in the Middle East. Our world, according to them, is in dire shape. I must say the media brings that news right into our homes and, I am sure, into many of our hearts. What more can I do to help the world?

As I wrote this, we were approaching Thanksgiving. I sat comfortably in a warm home with all the comforts one can need, even enough water to bathe and to have a cup of tea. I felt grateful. I counted my blessings. My daughter Ellen had just arrived from England, and my granddaughter Isabelle was spending the night. My whole family would be coming for the week and especially for Thursday. The turkey was in the fridge, and I couldn't wait to begin cooking. I love to make the pies. My husband loves to grill the turkey. It fills my heart and soul to recognize my bounty. I do not take for granted all I am blessed with, and from that bounty I have taken measures to help others, besides my prayers, although I do fervently believe that my prayers are the first and most important step. It's been shown that when many pray together for the same outcome, things do change for the better, including the prayer.

During this time my church, St. Michael the Archangel, was in the throes of putting together thousands of boxes of food to give away during Thanksgiving. We are but one of many organizations that do the same thing. We have a "Jesse Tree" in the foyer with paper ornaments with children's names who need a present, usually clothing. There are adopt-a-family notices in our bulletin. We are a country with an abundance of resources, and from what I can see here in my community, we want to share those with whomever needs help. As a family, we aren't ever generous enough. It seems no matter how much we donate or step up to assist others, we could always do more, more, and more. We aren't called to be missionaries working in the needy parts of the world. We are called, however, to be compassionate, and that means not just thinking sad thoughts but actually stepping up and making a difference. It means donating to the Thanksgiving Basket drive, taking at least one ornament off the Jesse Tree, spending time in service. It means recognizing our bounty and our blessings and making a difference. We want to donate our time, treasure, and talent to improve the condition of our world, even if it's just our small part of it.

After my day retreat, I also realized I need to be more caring of our planet. My first step was to realize I wasn't taking enough time to "smell the roses." So much of my day is spent running around doing that I've forgotten to embrace the beauty and appreciate the bounty of my planet. Growing up amid the highways, sidewalks, and brick buildings of a city was not the place to get in touch with nature. I did spend my summers on Jones Beach, and I fell in love with the ocean. I love the salt water and the waves and the sound, but it took a move to North Carolina before I was stopped in my tracks by nature. Perhaps, too, it's more about being older and getting closer to being reunited with the earth that has me paying more attention to its grandeur and miracles. My first step, therefore, was to slow down and to daily savor the miracles that surround me. Ah, another opportunity to meditate! My second step was to find more ways to sustain our resources, even if it's just me taking one small step: walk when I can, use less water more often, recycle even more fervently, don't print something I can save on the computer, plan my errands all at once rather than heading out randomly.

I am always looking for a way to be of more service to the world. In this case, our day retreat gave me a greater awareness of the responsibility to literally give back to Mother Earth, that planet which so tenderly holds us here. I used to have the affirmation "I treat Mother Earth gently," but now, with awareness I claim with more fervor, *"I recognize my responsibility to be a good steward of my Mother Earth."* Therefore, for Thanksgiving of 2014, I gave thanks for ALL things but especially for the treasures of our miraculous world.

10. Strengthening My Spirit

Affirmation: *I have a healthy spirit because I pay attention to those practices that strengthen it.*

As I write this, the United States is passing from celebrating the holiday of Thanksgiving to preparing for Christmas. Every year the space between Thanksgiving and Christmas gets smaller and smaller; actually, there is not any space unless you claim it, because retail begins Christmas right after Halloween. During this time there was a very sad cartoon in the paper. An older couple was standing at the head of an empty but fully set dining table. They had the roasted turkey on a platter and were ready to serve, but no one was there. The wife's comment was "We should have known what to expect when they announced the sales would begin on Thanksgiving Day." My good news was that except for my youngest daughter, who lives in England, our Thanksgiving table this year held the entire family, including my grandson Joe's fiancée.

My husband and I love Thanksgiving. We love any occasion that brings our family to our home and to our table. Sharing time and stories and our lives with the people we love the most is the highest blessing of our lives. It is heartwarming that our family responds in kind. They did not leave early to start their shopping or to go to the movies or to escape for any other reason. We shared the meal, had coffee and dessert, and then our grandson Sam played and sang three original songs he had written. My heart overflowed.

Madonna, the singer, prophesied what has become reality. We live in a material world. I am as guilty of liking and wanting nice things as anyone else. I love it when the house is all pretty inside. I like a new pair of shoes or a new outfit. I love a gadget or two. I like my comforts and my security, but my age puts me closer to the end of my life than the beginning, and I recognize that the material things of this world are not where my ultimate happiness lies.

My mom was in an assisted-living facility toward the end of her life. She was a strong ninety-one, but I watched her become more and more frail. I visited there often both to see her and to bring communion to the Catholic residents in the entire facility from the independent living to the Alzheimer's unit. It was a gift to me to share the lives of the residents even in such a small way. It made me aware of my phase of life and grateful for the stage I was in at that time.

"I worked on my external well-being in the early part of my life and recognized I needed to work on my internal well-being for the later part of my life." This was the statement from an older woman who hosted weekly gatherings at her home to examine different spiritual concepts. About fifteen women attended each week, and if the owner was away, someone else had her key so the group could still gather. What are you doing to work on your internal well-being? What steps need to be taken so that when you are no longer able to do all you want to do, you will still feel safe and comfortable and alive!

It's a fact that we all age differently. I've written before about one of my heroines, Eleanor Cioffi, my mother's best friend. At this time, she was still living alone, and many days when I'd arrive at the gym, she'd already be there working out on the weight machines. She'd adjust the machine, put her cane down, and then do her reps. One of the aerobics instructors told me she was shocked to see Eleanor's age on a form. "She's ninety-four," she claimed. I asked her to go back and redo the numbers. I knew that Eleanor had had a birthday that month. She was ninety-nine!

I want to be an Eleanor. I'm doing all in my power to stay as healthy as possible, and I know I am in charge of some of my physical well-being but not all of it. I know, too, that fate can be a life-changing influence, so I am working on strengthening my spiritual and emotional well-being as well.

I am always open to opportunities for inner growth. My yoga practice is an excellent exercise in being open and flexible. I often have people tell me how they "can't do yoga." They tell me they are not flexible enough. Yes, if they think yoga is about standing on your head or twisting up like a pretzel, they are right. But if one can breathe, one can do yoga. As the body changes, the practice can change. It is not a competitive sport. It's all about connecting your mind, body, and spirit. At one time you may have been able to do a handstand (or not) and that's nice, but now your practice may have a softer, more gentle feel. You're still breathing. You're still being aware. You're still connecting the three major elements of your being: mind, body, and spirit. The same may be true of your life as you age. You're still breathing. You're still aware. You can still connect the three major elements of your being. You just may need to do it in a different, perhaps a more gentle way than in the past.

Life is about growth and learning to adjust to change, but also thriving within it. One of the gentlemen I visited at Woodland Terrace bemoaned his physical limitations, but then he told me he had a new toy; he'd bought a computer and was learning to use it. He was excited by this whole new aspect to his life. It was helping him with his physical limitations. I am always inspired by those who adjust their life poses to accommodate their new circumstances and find joy and even excitement in their new position.

So, I not only continue to do physical exercise, I also added spiritual aerobics. I actively sought those practices that strengthen my emotional and spiritual muscles. I look for community that nurtures and inspires me. One of my favorite groups is a study group, the Seekers, where we discuss different self-help books. At the time of this writing, we have met twice a month for many years. When we discussed this topic of physical changes, one friend reminded me, "We can always talk." It's a gift for me to have the support of these friends in a safe, nonjudgmental environment. We work on our "internal well-being," and I do feel stronger and healthier because of our sharing and camaraderie.

Some of my other spiritual "push-ups" consist of prayer time, journaling, reading, connecting with friends and family, and always being open to new experiences. Whatever life throws at me, I am hoping and, yes, praying that I will have developed the strength and fortitude to pull myself up above the fray. If faced with an emotional marathon, I am hoping to have trained well enough to be able to cross the finish line regardless of my physical limitations. What nurtures your mind and spirit? Whatever it is, invest in it. Put your time, treasure, and talent into those practices that will enable you, too, to be internally strong and powerful.

11. Searching for Service

Affirmation: *I pray daily for those who most need God's mercy and open myself to be of service to whomever God sends me.*

Pope Francis, Jorge Mario Bergoglio, has inspired the world. He was elected Pope in April of the year following the historic resignation of Pope Benedict XVI. He didn't want to be Pope. He didn't expect to become the Pope. He had already purchased his return ticket for Argentina. Immediately after his election all sorts of tales began appearing in the news. It appears he is a very newsworthy person. One of the first stories was about him paying the bill for his hotel room himself and then taking a taxi back to where he needed to be. Now, I've done those things many times in my life, as I'm sure you have, but no one ever thought it was of so much interest that they announced it in the media! The behavior and words of Pope Francis have since been announced and scrutinized. He is both applauded and criticized. He is unlike most world leaders, and yet he is subject to the same scrutiny as all of them. He comes up short for some, but it appears as of this date, he is mostly being hailed as a man of humility and wisdom, two qualities we all should strive to possess but which if possessed by our leaders make for a kinder, more compassionate society.

In 2013 Pope Francis was named *Man of the Year* by *Time Magazine*. It appears the criteria for this acknowledgment is who *Time* determines has had the greatest impact on society during the year. It is not always someone who has had a positive effect on our world. The opposite is true for Pope Francis. They named him because of his philosophy regarding improving the world. His mission is to provide care and dignity for all human beings. Mother Teresa also had that mission. It's what Jesus Christ's mission was when He walked on this earth, and according to our Catholic tradition, Pope Francis is His representative here, today. He is the 266th Pope, and so far he has shown himself to be quite unique in his role. There's been a photo circulating on the Internet that shows Pope Francis in one half and Pope Benedict XVI in the other. It says,

"Can you see the difference?" Unlike the Sunday cartoon quiz which makes it difficult to pick out the differences, this "quiz" is very easy. Pope Francis has abandoned the fancy trappings used by the Popes of the past.

One of the other pictures circulated was of Pope Francis kissing the head of a severely disfigured man. There was a rumor that he went out into the slums of Italy and provided solace for the populace. It is a fact that he did do this when he was in Argentina, so it's not too far-fetched to believe he's continued this practice. His first encyclical addressed the distribution of wealth throughout the world. He doesn't believe the system in most countries, including ours in the United States, works to the benefit of the neediest. Conservatives who only focus on economics aren't very happy with the Pope's message, but the Pope isn't concerned with their opinion. He is only concerned with how society will respond to the needs of the most poor and the most suffering among us. Yes, I said "us."

In my daily reading of *Spiritual Insights for Daily Living* edited by Elizabeth Fenske, the focus for the month of December is unity. Each day I am reminded that we are all one. Once you begin to believe that, you will recognize that if one of us is suffering, we are responsible to find a way to alleviate that suffering. At the time of this entry, the world was suffering, of this there was no doubt. It takes very little awareness to recognize the distress of this world. Sometimes when I hear some of the stories, I am completely overwhelmed by what's going on. I am horrified by the cruelty. I fully recognize that I don't even have a clue of the horrors that are taking place in our world even as I write this, and to be honest, I really don't want to know the details. I only know they exist, and as this particular year passed, I found myself called to step up and to be more aware of the poor and suffering and to reach out in a way that alleviates their suffering, perhaps even brings them joy and peace.

It was the message I was receiving at this time. It began before Pope Francis was even elected. It had been here all along as all important messages are, but I wasn't ready to fully embrace it. I mean what can I do to help those most in need? The second part of that question is, what will I be called on to do, and am I ready and willing? The clearest message came from Albert Haase's book *Catching Fire, Becoming Flame*. He says that focusing on Christ "leads us right into the heart of a suffering, needy world where we are sent to respond lovingly to the unmet need or required duty of the present moment." It is our mission in life. It is our reason for existing, to make the world a kinder, more compassionate place.

As my friend and I walked around the lake, we talked about how we could help change the world. It was a good walk! What can we possibly do to aid in the conversion of hearts to bring them to a place of love and peace? We can begin with ourselves. The first place where the transformation must begin is within our own hearts. Luke 1:68-79 says, "Let there be peace on earth and let it begin with me." After that the soul is open to the flame of transformation. If you take some time every day to connect to the Divine, you will be led to opportunities to ease the suffering of another, of others. The opportunity is there. There are so many ways to be of service if one is asking to receive them.

A friend of mine once stopped to talk to a man who looked quite deranged and was obviously homeless. She asked him how he was doing and engaged him in a nice discussion. The rest of us had quickly walked past. Afterward I asked her why she had done that. She told me she asked God every day to send people to her who were in need and to whom she could respond. She told me she never knew where they would appear, and she couldn't take the chance of passing someone by who might be an answer to her prayers. Do you think her kind words made any difference?

A study that took place in NYC had two groups of people on a busy sidewalk. One group would nod and smile at passersby. The other group would ignore the pedestrians. The researchers then asked one person a few questions about how they were feeling. (How they got someone in NYC to stop and chat with them was amazing to me.) The people who were smiled at had a higher level of contentment than those who were ignored. If a simple smile from a stranger can add to the joy of this world, what kind of a difference can we make if we are making an effort to ease the suffering and pain of whomever we meet and, hopefully, whomever we are holding in our prayers?

Trust me, just like my friend, once you ask God to allow you to be of service, opportunities will present themselves. And once you open yourself up to caring about the marginalized and suffering of this world, not only will you make a difference in other's lives, you will make a difference in your life. Your heart and this world will be transformed.

12. Believing in Miracles

Affirmation: *I believe in miracles.*

In Rachel Remen's book *The Will to Live and Other Mysteries*, she offers up the opinion that most people are more concerned with mastery than with mystery. She goes on to give examples of events she and others have experienced that cannot be explained with science or with logic. But if one is open to believing in the unbelievable, the events not only take on meaning; they become powerful examples of spirit alive and at work in the world and in our lives.

My Christian faith is grounded in mystery. At some point I had to decide to believe the unbelievable. Let's admit it, the whole story of Jesus Christ's birth, death, and resurrection is pure mystery. If I were to assume that with my limited intelligence—or anyone's, even the brilliant—I am able to understand God, I would not only be arrogant but stupid. For heaven's sake, we may one day completely understand our own bodies, but we will never be able to duplicate them. Only Divine power could have created a human being. We may one day be able to travel the Universe, but will we ever reach its outer limits? Sir Arthur Eddington, British astronomer, physicist, and mathematician of the early twentieth century, said, "The universe is not only stranger than we imagined, but stranger than we can imagine." David Finkelstein, a brilliant physicist, said, "We haven't the capacity to imagine anything crazy enough to stand a chance of being right." We are human and so we are limited in our understanding, but we are also spirit, made in God's image and likeness, and therefore we can tap into, connect to the unknown and perhaps even rest in it.

I have discovered that in order to be at peace, I need to embrace the mystery of my faith and the mystery of life. I choose to believe in a personal God, one who can work miracles in my life, one who is listening to my dreams, concerns, and petitions and even the whispers of my heart if I stay close, open, and present.

I am not aware of any personal acquaintances who have experienced significant miracles. I wish I were. Certainly, I have read about others who have, and when my husband and I visited St. Joseph's Oratory of Mount Royal in Montreal, I was stunned by the hundreds and hundreds of crutches hanging on the walls that were left by people who had come there for a miracle and found one. Once I Googled "miracle locations," and one site, ListVerse.com, listed the top ten recorded miracles. You may recognize some of the more well-known: Fatima, Lourdes, Our Lady of Guadeloupe, and more recently Padre Pio. All of these places and events are known for the unexplainable. Lourdes, the site of the appearance of the Blessed Mother to St. Bernadette, has sixty-eight "official" miracles and thousands of unofficial healings.

Are the healings simply the result of the power of positive thinking? People really believe it will happen and so it does? Could be. So what? Something miraculous occurred. Maybe that's the secret to miracles; if we are open to them, if we truly believe, "even as a grain of mustard seed" our beings are transformed into receptors for miracles.

Notice I have a tendency to focus on the illogical positive experiences that happen to people; this is, after all, a book for creating positive affirmations. I avoid focusing on the occult or unsettling things one might hear about or see in the media. Those don't help me in any way to feel hopeful, peaceful, or grounded. It's my choice what to focus on. I know there is evil in the world.

The news that was coming into my life at this time was unsettling. There had been multiple requests for prayers for the suffering and struggles of friends and friends of friends. In two cases acquaintances who did not appear to be ill were diagnosed with cancer and given less than three weeks to live. I had a scare during my annual mammogram when a lump was found and I was sent for an ultrasound. It turned out to be normal tissue, but it shook me to the core. Besides deciding to eat French fries and a cookie, *carpe diem*, I needed a way to find peace with the whims of the world and so I did what I had been practicing, I rested in my faith. I don't know what the future holds other than death, and I don't understand most of what life is about, but once again, if I connect to the Divine, to my God, I find I can simply allow life to be and allow myself to be at peace with all as it is, at least at that very moment.

When I went through my yoga teacher training, we were invited to "rest in the inquiry." We were encouraged during our practice not to try to figure everything out, but to simply let our asanas (poses) unfold. I've taken that practice into my faith. I'm doing my utmost to shed Divine light on life and into other lives, perhaps even into the world. I'm offering us an opportunity to let go of our egos, especially mine, and to allow my Loving Father, my Lord and Savior Jesus Christ, His Holy Spirit, our Blessed Mother, my guardian angel, and all those unseen entities who want to guide me and you to a richer, peaceful, blessed life the opportunity to do so. So I decided to allow Spirit to inhabit my heart, soul, and body. I invited it in and I chose to simply rest with it. I know I don't know and that's okay with me.

I know in today's world this is a path less chosen, but one of my yearly intentions was to "connect to the Divine," and my life's intention is to strengthen my faith. With those intentions in place, I chose to focus on mystery and to release myself from trying to understand all things. Once I adopted that approach, even the unexplainable became meaningful and God's presence became more real. Along with this gift I'd given myself, even the great unknown, the future and the greatest unknown, life after death became less fearful, less anxiety producing, and I found I could still breathe and live peacefully, at least for that moment. And really, isn't that all we have, that one moment?

13. Why Be Vulnerable?

Affirmation: *By going outside of my comfort zone, I empower myself.*

When I first moved to North Carolina in 1986, my neighbor invited me to walk with her. I'd always been physically active. I skated as a child, both ice and roller. I climbed trees, jumped rope, played ball, and rode a bike to name just a few activities. As a young adult I played tennis, but I had never exercised for the sake of exercising. This invitation was inviting me to try something new. My neighbor also wanted me to walk with her three mornings a week at 5:00. I love the mornings and I've always risen at a fairly early hour, but to get up when it was still dark and to be dressed and out the door and walking the streets was quite a challenge. We were to walk several miles, and initially I was not physically prepared. I needed to ice my shins after each walk because of shin splints—sharp pains in the front of my calves. After a couple of weeks, however, the shin splints disappeared and I started to look forward to our chats. After a short time, a few of the other neighbors joined us, and now we were not only exercising our bodies but building our community.

I moved from that neighborhood in 1990, but walking has become an essential part of my quest to be optimally healthy. I do not at this time, however, walk at 5:00 a.m. When I wrote this I had the luxury of heading out after the sun had risen. The decision to say yes to my young neighbor's invitation was a life-changing one. The experience not only opened my world to the importance of exercise, but it empowered me by allowing me to see what I could accomplish if I decided to unite my mind and my body.

I had stepped outside of my comfort zone. It may seem like a small step, but for me, it was a giant leap. It was the beginning of a lifetime pursuit of staying strong and healthy. It certainly wasn't the first time I had been outside my comfort zone. When I first arrived in North Carolina, I was already forty years old. I'd moved many times, had three children, and had taught for several years, but somehow this challenge to walk was different. Accepting and meeting this challenge of weekly walks was life-changing. Perhaps I didn't think I could make such a commitment, but I did and once I allowed myself to be proud of this feat, I found myself wondering of what else I was capable. I guess, looking back on it, it was one of the most empowering decisions of my life.

Every day we are faced with decisions, small and large, important and trivial, but each decision shapes our lives and shapes our future. Certainly, I can look back on my life and see how some choices enhanced my life, and I can see how if I had chosen differently how very different my life would be today. We are not only charged with making choices that will benefit our lives; we are then charged with making a conscious choice to mentally frame that choice in a positive light, to make sure that the consequences of that decision enhances our lives. It would be easy to do if it were a choice that led to some perceived blessing, but when the decision leads to a struggle or perhaps even a disaster, reframing it can prove to be extremely difficult. But with practice, it can be done, even if it's simply to use the experience as a lesson which empowers us going forward.

The second focus of Brené Brown's *Daring Greatly* is vulnerability (the first focus was about shame, which I wrote about in the entry *Shame on You!*). "When we allow ourselves to be vulnerable we open ourselves up to making mistakes but we also open ourselves up to opportunity and growth. One must walk the fine line between humility and foolishness if one is to embrace the quality of vulnerability." What Brené Brown writes about is the opportunity to live a full, rich life because we are not afraid to try something that makes us uncomfortable, to try something at which we might fail. That behavior not only takes us outside of our comfort zone, but it encourages the virtue of humility.

What would we try if one weren't afraid to fail, if we were willing to be vulnerable? It's not only what we might learn but who we might become. I have some of the most amazing friends. People who are not just willing to try something new but look for opportunities to do so. My only concern is that sometimes they don't see what remarkable things they are doing. They don't or won't take credit for their awesome spirits. Sure, there are historical accounts of people whose humility changed the world, people like Abraham Lincoln and Mahatma Gandhi, but I love to look at those heroes who are in my immediate life and relish their virtues. There are so very many.

There are the writers who open up their lives to others. The painters who display their work. There are those who start their own businesses. I have friends who have done mission trips to all different parts of the world. How about those friends who begin a new career in their retirement years? Some of the most remarkable women I've ever met are the ones who attend the Pink Ribbon Yoga Retreat (the Duke-sponsored retreat for women breast cancer survivors), especially the ones who come knowing no one and without a clue of where they are going or what they'll be doing. I'm sure you can think of many people in your life who step outside of their comfort zones. They may not initially think they can, but that doesn't stop them; they do it anyway. They know they might fail, but they also know they might succeed. They might feel fear but don't let it deter them. It doesn't matter one way or the other because just by saying, "Yes," simply by being willing to be vulnerable, to be humble, their lives will be richer and more rewarding.

Yes, it was a small step to agree to walk at 5:00 three mornings a week. We need not take huge steps to initiate change in our lives. The little "yeses" are the beginnings which empower us to one day take a giant step and maybe not only change our world but the world.

WINTER

1. Christmas Miracles

Affirmation: *I possess the Christmas spirit all year long.*

Miracle on 34th Street was released in May of 1947. It originally had the word "Christmas" in the title, but because of the release date, it was removed. How do I know this? When my husband, Sandy, and I went to visit his mom, Yolanda, in Savannah, Georgia, they were having a fund-raiser at the local original Savannah Movie Theatre showing *Miracle on 34th Street*. We had all seen it many times and we knew it was delightful, but we went anyway to simply share the afternoon together and to support the Humane Society. Once again, I was wrong! Watching this classic, corny movie in the midst of a crowded theatre was a remarkably different experience than watching it at home alone or in a small group. We laughed, sighed, applauded, and shared all the clever and tender moments that have kept this film so meaningful.

It's definitely a secular film. There is no mention of a God or Christ, other than in the frequently used word "Christmas," but what I consider to be the spirit of Christmas permeates every scene. Do you recall the movie? Kris Kringle, the "real" Santa Claus, is only about making others feel valued, loved, and important. It's not about the physical gifts Macys has told to promote; it's what they represent to the child or adult who is asking for them. He brings people together for their betterment and the betterment of all. He spreads his charm and goodwill like a net over everyone with whom he comes into contact. He converts the unbelieving, skeptical Maureen O'Hara and her disenchanted child, Natalie Wood, into people with imagination and faith. He even converts the USPS.

I once saw a cartoon in *USA Today* where two children were standing in front of Santa asking for "world peace and goodwill towards men." He asked them if they'd consider an Xbox instead. The news during the week of this missive was so sad and tragic that I couldn't listen, but that doesn't seem uncommon anymore. It only took a glance at the headlines to see the horror we were perpetuating on our fellow human being. Had the devil won? Had "Satan" truly become the ruler of this world? It would be so easy to believe we were at the end of times, but it was Christmas. Christmas is a time to promote hope, peace, and love for everyone, whether one is or is not labeled "Christian." We know what He came to do. He came to show the world that we were put here to love and to serve, and that, I believe, is the one true truth. He was here to raise our level of awareness to a higher purpose. He wasn't concerned with the rules and regulations. He was only concerned with the person and his or her well-being. He was here to bring comfort to those who most needed it and to make uncomfortable those who are able to be of comfort.

I know there are many believers who believe theirs is the only way. There's the joke about the Catholic, Baptist, Mormon, you choose, who arrives in heaven and asks St. Peter why he whispers every time he gets close to this huge wall. Why is there a wall at all? St. Peter tells them that the Catholics, Baptists, Mormons, you choose, are on the other side of the wall and "They believe they are the only ones up here." Oh, to be so sure. To know that because you are right, you are saved and the rest of the world is damned; how truly sad. I read a wonderful quote recently: "You can be right or you can love."

One of my greatest strengths is my gift of perseverance. I believe it's the reason I have accomplished most things in my life. I truly believe if I simply "hang in there," I will learn or finish whatever it is I'm working upon. The other side of perseverance is stubbornness, and I am as guilty of that as I am proud of my determination. Just ask my hubby. For example, one summer, I wanted to walk a new path around a lake in the North Carolina mountains. We headed out and after an hour we hadn't reached the lake yet. Sandy reasonably wanted to turn around. Turn around! I couldn't even imagine it. We hadn't even seen the lake yet! Finally, a few minutes later we arrived. I knew we were close. I was right! Now he reasonably wanted to go back the way we had come. Go back the same way? No, no, no! We needed to follow the path and head up the other way. I had been told it was the same distance. I knew I was right! He agreed and we got lost, and four hours later, we finally found our way to our starting point.

Sandy not only didn't leave me, he barely scolded me. He lives a life of love, not right. It wasn't the first time he's had to put up with my set thinking, and I am here to confess he is not the only person in my life with whom I've exhibited this trait. It's one of those personality shadows that interferes with the quality of my relationships and which I have only recently begun to understand. Perhaps this is why I've been granted these many years of life, so I can continue to recognize how flawed I truly am. What was Pope Francis' first message? "I am a sinner, pray for me." Oh, yes, we are all flawed, but as long as we don't believe we are above or beyond anyone else, we can embrace our humanness and know that God created us just as we are. She/He created the miracles of this universe, and we are, each one of us, one of those miracles.

Christmas is not an easy holiday for many, many people, but perhaps it's because the true meaning has been lost. Christ is coming, God. He comes again and again every year, and I believe He remains with all those who choose to love, care, and be of service to the world. The Christ the Savior is here in the hearts of all who know the importance of spreading the net of compassion and love over everyone whose lives they touch. That miracle on 34th Street is the miracle that can be ours should we choose to open our minds and our hearts to The Christ.

May you always have a blessed holiday season and a life filled with the awareness of God's love.

2. A Year of Love

Affirmation: *I am fully open to love, human and divine. Love surrounds me and permeates every aspect of my existence.*

When I went to visit Paul, I noticed the wedding pictures on his wall. He was one of the few men in the Alzheimer's unit and he was a flirt. He was good-looking, tall and lean, and always had on a baseball cap. He was in the beginning stages, and I could easily have a conversation with him. Then I also noticed the memorial card with what I guessed was his wife's name. I asked him if I was correct and if the card referred to his wife. It did. "Were you married a long time?" I asked. I didn't really expect an answer. I was just making conversation. "Sixty-one years," he replied. "Wow!" I responded. "That's a long time." He came right back at me, "Not long enough!" That was many years ago, but even as I wrote this my heart ached and my eyes teared up. "Not long enough." What a lesson! It came at me like a speeding train and left me dazed by the side of the tracks. Life is precious and, for so very many, "not long enough."

One of my dear friends lost her mother to Alzheimer's. It was a long, difficult battle. My friend lived in North Carolina, but her "mum" lived in England. She would often fly over to visit and to care for her mother. When her mother was finally admitted to a care facility, my friend when visiting would get up every morning, take the bus, and spend the entire day visiting and helping with the other residents. The facility eventually offered her a job. Her mother stopped recognizing her daughter, but one day she told my friend, "I don't know who you are, but I know you love me very much."

"I know you love me very much." "Not long enough." Words emanating from a place deep within, nothing trite or superficial; the murmurings of the heart, not just of the mind. When I looked at my life, searched my soul, what heart murmurs did I hear? And if I lost my mind, would the messages be about love? I dedicated my 68th year as

The Year of Love.

My church, the Catholic Church, dedicates each year to some worthy theme: *The Year of Faith* or *The Year of the Eucharist*, etc. Why not let it be an example for me and dedicate a year of my life to some worthy concept? *The Year of Love!* It's my ultimate goal, to love deeply, unconditionally, nonjudgmentally, and without attachment. It's the work of a lifetime. It seems worthwhile and appropriate to take at least a year to focus on love.

One more Alzheimer's story: In the video for the song "Raymond" by Brett Eldredge, an elderly woman has the mistaken idea that the maintenance man is her deceased son, Raymond. The video shows that Raymond died in the Vietnam War, but Kathryn, the lady in the video, has no memory of that. Her memory only goes back to 1943. She's a blessed woman. She appears comfortable in her surroundings, and the cleaning man is kind and gracious. "I bring her morning coffee every day," he sings. "Sometimes I find myself wishing I'd been there." He seems to love her, this woman who believes he is her son. He knows she loves him. It's such a small act of kindness, but it's such a grand act of love. The video reflects love in its purest form. It seems to seep from the screen out into the room. I never fail to weep when I watch it.

What is more important than creating a life filled with love? Once we can learn to accept love, we can more generously give love. We may not like everyone—that's a given—but it is possible to still love them or at least to hold them in a space of love. You can pray for your worst enemy, and I don't mean for evil to invade their lives. It is possible to find a place in our hearts to ask for the best for everyone in the world, those we find easy to love and those who challenge us. Remember, you can't make your world any brighter by blowing out someone else's light. The heart is a muscle. If we want it to become strong and healthy, we have to exercise it just like any other muscle.

If I lose my mind, which I must confess seems more threatening some days than others, I want to know that my heart is still full of love and my body—my spirit—is filled with the blessings of a life filled with love. I want to live a life where I can say, "Not long enough." A life where one day someone will look at me and say, "I know you love me." Hopefully, they will also know who I am and I will recognize them.

3. Setting an Intention

Affirmation: *This year is dedicated as "The Year of Divine Connection."*

It was the beginning of a new year when this was written. I had already visited and examined the past year and I now wanted to look forward. Of course, I didn't know what whims of fate would await me, but I had stocked the toolbox with tons of coping skills, so I was not going to go forward in fear. I was going forward in faith and with joyful expectation. What would you expect from someone who writes about Positive Affirmations?

The previous year was a good year. When I answered the first question on my review list about the hardest thing I had to do, the answer wasn't all that difficult. It was a lot better than some years, that's for sure. After I wrote the answer, I actually felt myself smiling at how very blessed I felt.

Many years ago I owned a refrigerator-size calendar that had the entire year on one piece of paper. I loved that calendar. I loved looking at the whole year ahead and planning our adventures and special occasions. I still like to look at the year ahead, but now it's all on my computer. Somehow it doesn't feel as satisfying, but I've adjusted.

Taking an intention is a regular part of a yoga practice. I've expanded that to my "off the mat" practice. I sometimes take an intention for the day. It's pretty cool when it appears in my daily journal. We take an intention each year for the Pink Ribbon Yoga Retreat (a Duke Hospital-sponsored retreat for women breast cancer survivors). The committee has always discussed what they'd like to focus on, and the intention usually comes quite quickly. The first year I decided to set a personal intention for the whole year was 2013. As I shared earlier, that was the year I declared "The Year of Love."

I have always loved the color yellow. Our homes have always had a lot of yellow in them. I've been accused of living in a yellow "submarine." It makes me feel happy and yet I still feel grounded when I'm in a yellow room. Not all yellows, however; it's more buttery than gold. I've usually added other colors to punch it up, like hot pink or purple. For the last few months of 2013, I had an attraction to the color green. I mention this because it was a new phase. Previously I had avoided green. There wasn't any green inside my home or in my wardrobe. First I painted my office apple green. Then I added a Kelly green print to a couch and then I went crazy and chose green granite for the renovated kitchen. Nothing I had in the former kitchen went with the green color, but I was irresistibly drawn to it. I just relaxed and let it happen. Why, I wondered, was this shift taking place? I was discussing my intention for 2013 with a dear friend and healer, Blaire Schultz, and mentioned my new bent toward the green color. She reminded me about the chakra colors. Guess what color the heart chakra is! Yup, it's green.

I'd like to believe that my dedication to The Year of Love led to more than just an attraction to green and a new decorating scheme. Personal growth and internal development is a slow process. It's just like most other changes one is attempting. They take time. There are subtle differences that may not even be perceived for a long time. It's like that with our affirmations. We choose them carefully, write them, read them, perhaps say them to ourselves and let them slowly permeate our subconscious and eventually our cellular structure. Then one day we respond to a situation differently than we had in the past, in a way that affirms us, not diminishes us, and we realize our affirmation has manifested.

As I looked forward to 2014, I had trouble deciding what besides love was important enough to focus on for a whole year. I thought about choosing faith as a focus and I considered forgiveness, but neither of those felt right. I did, however, want to keep a focus on forgiveness. One of my affirmations is *I freely forgive myself and others*. And I always want my faith to grow.

I attended a retreat many years ago with my friend Ann Baucom and her spiritual director. I was going over those notes at one point, and there was the spiritual direction for which I was looking. It entreated me to let my faith grow, not because of a sense of obedience or even a sense of belonging, but because it is rooted in experience. Faith doesn't only increase because of our religious experiences, although it is possible. But for many, me included, faith experiences happen both in and outside of church, and that's exactly what I want. I want to see the moon and the stars. I want to feel the sun warm my skin. I want to relish holding someone's hand. I want to hear the bird's song and the ocean's roar, and I want in that experience to feel God's presence. I want to feel connected to the Divine. I'd like to be connected at all times, but this is a meditation, a practice. In order to achieve this relationship, this intention, I need to pay close attention and focus on my ultimate desire. Yes, that is something I would be willing to spend a year cultivating, even a lifetime. So I dedicated 2014 as The Year of Connecting to the Divine.

What are you willing to dedicate a year of your life toward? Perhaps it's not one phrase; perhaps you have a list of intentions. I have one of them too. It reminds me of God's bounty and of the truth that I cannot fathom the riches that can be found once we connect to the Divine. My ideal life always includes optimal health, but good health and an ideal life require more than care for the body, which will cease to exist one day no matter how well I care for it. I need to focus on the spirit too. As in the past I carefully considered what my ideal life would include. I have carefully crafted ten intentions.

Pray Unceasingly
Forgive Continually
Accept and Give Love Freely
Hug Whenever Possible
Learn Constantly
Dance Often
Eat Mindfully
Recognize the Shadows
Smile Early, Laugh Daily
Be Grateful, Always and for All Things

May your life also be filled with abundant blessings, prosperity, and joy. Take some time and write down your intentions. Won't it be wonderful when you do your year-end review to find you've manifested your dreams and aspirations?

4. Just Breathe

Affirmation: *When I focus on my breath, I feel calmer.*

Jill Stockman led the class. It was at the third annual Yoga Fest in Raleigh, North Carolina. This was Howie Shareff's inspiration. He headed an organization called "You Call This Yoga," and his organization was sponsoring this event. There were over five hundred people attending the day-long workshop, and I had been "called" to be one of them. I hadn't felt any inclination to attend either of the first two, but the message had come through to me loud and clear that I was supposed to be at this year's Yoga Fest. I didn't know anyone else who was attending and I had a trip the next day I needed to pack for, but that interior voice was screaming at me, "Go, you need to go!" And so I did.

I would be taking four classes over the course of the day and I didn't know one teacher from the other. The classes all looked interesting, and I know I can always learn something new from any experience, so it didn't really matter to me which class I took. I decided to trust that whichever class in which I found myself would be exactly the class I was supposed to take.

The first class was good, very good. The room was packed and I was reminded of a breathing technique I had not consistently applied to my practice. Nice! The next class was titled "Finding Your Edge." I wasn't really sure I wanted to participate in a dynamic flow class, which is what I assumed this class would be, but I was signed up for it and following my own advice, I decided to stay for it. It was not good; it was inspirational. Jill was a master teacher. She was young and wispy and confident, and all that is nice, but those are not the qualities that make a teacher a master. She was wise and she clearly imparted her wisdom in a concise, universal language. This, I knew, was why I had been led to come to Yoga Fest. Where was my recorder?

Jill began by reminding us to take a full, deep breath and to fill our lungs and chest; to have a deliberate exhale with a reminder to draw in our belly buttons to our spine and engage our Mula Bandha (the pelvic floor). We then went on with some Kapalabhati (short repetitive inhales and one long exhale) breathing, she incorporated several series of Ohms and she then ended with another round of Kapalabhati. I felt an internal shift take place. I "returned" to Kripalu, the home of my training and a place where I had absorbed the positive, calming energy of the yoga practice.

The breath is the foundation of life. We begin life with our first inhale and we end life with our last exhale, and yet how many times during our day do we even notice our breathing? A dear friend gave me a plaque one day that said, "Things I need to do today: Breathe." One of the most important yogic tools is the breath. There are dozens of different types of breathing; some are slow and deep, others are more like panting, and some require one to hold one nostril closed and alternate between the two. Yoga is not just a series of poses or asanas. The ancient writings of Patanjali, the father of yoga, describes eight limbs or disciplines involved in the practice of yoga. The breathing or Pranayama is one of them. They all interweave with each other. When you unite your breath with your movements, you unite your mind with your body and with your spirit. It's a very powerful tool. I like to start my yoga classes by inviting the practitioners to watch their breath. "Watch the rise and the fall, the in and the out, the up and the down. Do not judge. There's no right or wrong, no good or bad. Just notice." Calm penetrates the atmosphere of the room. It's palpable. I decided I was at Jill's class to be reminded of how powerful life can be when I choose to focus on my breath.

In the ten-week course on Mindful Meditation at Duke's Integrative Medicine, the main teaching is how to calm the mind and therefore the body by simply sitting quietly and watching the breath. The basic teaching is to "watch" the breath and when thoughts come along, which they always do, notice them, release them, and go back to watching your breath. Most meditation practices focus on the breath. Many practices also invite you to create a mantra, a word that you can repeat over and over. I'd like to claim to be a devoted meditator but I am not. I pray, I journal, but I have only meditated sporadically, not religiously, even though I truly believe it's one of the best paths to optimal mental and physical health. When I have meditated and searched for a mantra, I found myself focusing on the word "Jesus." My inhale led me to "Jees" and my exhale to "us." Then I realized that even if I'm not in a meditative state, I'm always breathing and I could use my mantra any time I stopped and took a deep breath, "Jesus." It was a short prayer that brought me home to my God. Now, all I needed to do was to put the exercise into practice, to make a conscious choice to take that deep breath whenever I possibly could, whenever I would think to do so.

The focus of my daily reading during the month of February in *Spiritual Insights for Daily Living,* edited by Elizabeth Fenske, is on meditation. Actually, all of the self-help books I've ever picked up have at least one section devoted to meditation. At this time I was reading Richard Rohr's *The Naked Now.* He, too, speaks about the breath. He explains that the Hebrew term for God, Yahweh, is believed to be derived from four sounds—Yod Hay Vov Hay—the sound of breathing. It was such a sacred sound, the name of God, that the Hebrews rarely spoke it. They didn't need to speak it; they honored God, brought God to them, into them with every breath. The breath is the life-giving force which sustains us and which, if we choose, can keep us connected to the Divine.

I figured out that I was "called" to Yoga Fest for several reasons, some of which I did not even recognize. One of the reasons, I believe, was to help me refocus on the importance of paying attention to my breathing. I had had a really rough start in 2014 and I'd lost touch with my breathing practice. It was a wonderful gift to receive from Jill and the other yoga instructors. It's interesting to me how often my yoga practice helps me to strengthen my faith and reconnect with my God. It's amazing that something so simple, breathing, can be so complex and so very powerful. Join me, "Take a deep breath, exhale fully. Again, one more time." **When I focus on my breath, I feel calmer, and when I am very attentive to it, I recognize I am connected to the Divine.**

5. Letting Go of Struggle

Affirmation: *I let go of struggle.*

In the winter of 2015, the Immaculate Conception parish in Durham, NC, held its annual women's retreat at the Baptist retreat center on Oak Island, North Carolina. Approximately fifty women attended. They were of all ages and ethnic backgrounds. There was one man, Father Jude Siciliano, but as one of the women tried to explain to me, he was such a remarkable man that the women attending would be very comfortable with his presence. She was right, very right.

I am quite familiar with creating and presenting retreats. The year 2015 was to be our eleventh Pink Ribbon Yoga Retreat. At the time of this entry, our first planning session was about to take place. It takes a solid six months to get an event like ours together.

The committee for the Immaculate Conception retreat also works on their event for many months beforehand. It was very obvious. They didn't miss a thing. It was everything I'd want a spiritual retreat to be. The design was very gentle with lots of free time. The rooms were comfortable and well-appointed. The setting was originally Fort Caswell with remnants of the cement bunkers and walls in the midst of lovely houses and stunningly beautiful ocean vistas. We were able to watch the sunrise and the sunset. The theme was "Reclaiming the Gifts of Sabbath Living," and we were encouraged to come with something written out that we wanted to eliminate from our lives. We were then encouraged to "take an intention" to help us accomplish our desire. I was right at home. I must admit I also felt a little smug; I mean, I'd already looked at the year and I had set an intention. I was ready! I really was, but just like all adventures, there was so much more to experience than I could even imagine.

We were a carpool of four—the only four from our part of the Research Triangle. It was a delightful ride to the beach. One of the other women took on all the driving and another coordinated our pickups. I was honored to be with these three spiritual sages. They had all worked hard at getting in touch with God, each in their own way. I couldn't wait to see what I would learn from each of them. The simple fact that I was not in charge of any aspect of this trip, other than packing my own suitcase, was a gift in itself. What a way to start a new year, in the company of three loving, wise women and then to share in the journey of several dozen other women all with the same desire to know God better, to find a way to be better connected to the Divine.

Father Jude led us in several ceremonies, but for me the most meaningful were the two Centering Prayer sessions, twenty minutes of eyes closed and emptying the mind. How easy that sounds but how difficult to put into practice. I've meditated now on and off, mostly off, for over thirty years. I'm great at praying and of course I always journal, but being called upon to just sit silently, without going to sleep, for twenty minutes, twice a day, is simply something I haven't made happen in my life, probably because I really don't want to. I am a busy person. There is so much to do and to think about and of which to be in charge! I do fully realize, however, the multiple benefits of meditation, of resting the brain and in this case in finally being silent so that I can listen to God, not always to be dominating the conversation. That's what we were given, two twenty-minute sessions to simply listen. Did God speak to me? Yes, She did!

During both sessions I received images that I cannot explain. I went into the first session with a question to which I could not find an answer, and somewhere in that twenty minutes, an answer came—one I felt I never would have arrived at using any other modality. I was actually stunned and felt a great sense of peace. During the second session I was prepared to simply sit quietly and repeat my word or "mantra," but once again I was visited with an image. It was a warm, comforting person and I was so grateful for her care. I might have stayed longer but the bell rang and she left. She left and yet I still felt her with me. I'm not sure if or when she will ever leave again.

I was curious now. Would each time in Centering Prayer bring a new insight, a warm feeling, a sense of peace and calm, or was it the power of almost fifty other people sitting with me that presented me with these gifts? As I mentioned before, at one time I took a ten-week course in Mindful Meditation at Duke Integrative Medicine. I sat quietly in lotus position, crossed legs, on the floor twice a day for twenty minutes for ten weeks and then the course ended and so did my practice. I know all the benefits meditation presents. I've read about lowering blood pressure, increasing self-discipline, improving concentration, and how the brain actually changes its state with ongoing meditation. In January of 2015, there was a *60 Minutes* episode that showed a computer scan of the beneficial effects on the brain during meditation. At the time of this writing, I was listening to Richard Rohr's *The Art of Letting Go*. I had just begun session four. Guess what the topic was? Contemplation or meditation and why it's so beneficial not only to our bodies but to our spirits.

Was I ready? Could I do it? Even as I wrote this, I could feel the resistance. "Be careful what you pray for," I've been told. So, I didn't ask God to help me with this intention. Instead I simply decided to allow the time to unfold and present itself to me. My intention for this year had already been set before I ever got to the retreat. It was The Year of Trusting in Christ. The quality I left behind at the retreat to honor Sabbath living was "struggle." My affirmation was ***I let go of struggle***, even the struggle to meditate daily. I decided simply to see how the days evolved and maybe this time, with God in the picture, my desire to sit quietly and discover His or Her message would come as a welcome gift.

Maybe you want to join me in this journey? I'd love to hear about what you discover.

6. An Awesome Life

Affirmation: *I choose awesome!*

As I wrote this it was toward the beginning of a new year. Many people shared with me their goals or resolutions. One person when describing her expectation of the next year used the word "awesome!" Another told me she always gets excited at the beginning of a year with all the possibilities that will be presented to her. Certainly we get to choose how we want to imagine our unknown future. I have one person in my life who says she doesn't imagine the future at all. She simply allows it to unfold; there's no expectation of any sort. Do you think that's actually possible? She must be making plans for some things, and she, I would imagine, is planning for a good or at least a pleasant outcome. When we start out on an adventure—and yes, a new year (even a new day) is the beginning of an adventure—we will normally carry in our minds and hearts some sense of anticipation. When the angels appeared to the shepherd to announce the beginning of Jesus' life here on Earth, they heralded, "Be not afraid." They were offering them a choice and guiding them to be at peace. Our response to what happens to us is in most respects what we get to choose. We may be anxious about the unknown, but we can choose to be excited or filled with fear.

Once again I was attending the Immaculate Conception women's retreat and I found myself pondering the question of how to hold the future events of my life in a positive, blessed light. I began by trying to believe that everything that will happen to me will be for my good. While that may be true, the real truth is there are some things I would rather avoid, even if they are for my good. I guess it's like not wanting to require medicine in order to get over some illness or even not having to eat kale in order to stay healthy. When unpleasant things arise and someone shares with me that it's probably for my benefit, I think of my husband Sandy's expression when he says, "That's like practicing bleeding." It's not something anyone wants to deal with. So, I began to go around asking people how they make peace with all the aspects of their lives, those we label "bad" or "disagreeable" or worst of all "disastrous."

The Seekers, one of my study groups, usually does a year-end review together, and we present a few questions to help shape the vision of the future year. This year we have chosen several questions from Sarah Susanka, renowned architect and author of *The Not So Big House* and *The Not So Big Life*, to promote a workshop she was presenting in Chapel Hill. I share them here for your perusal:

What has inspired you over the past year?

What were your sorrows and disappointments from the year, and how have you been changed by them?

What were your enthusiasms, accomplishments, creations, and joys, and how have you been changed by them?

What new patterns of behavior have you adopted over the past year, and what effects have they had?

How are you different this year than you were last year at this time?

Are there any things you are being asked to do right now that you are rejecting?

What recent synchronicities do you recall?

To what part of yourself are you giving birth?

Specifically what is it that you wish to focus on or experience in the coming year?

Father Jude Siciliano was again our retreat facilitator. He leads gently, not with commands but with a soft voice and reflective questions and readings. This year he opened the first session with Rumi's "The Guest House."

> *This being human is a guest house.*
> *Every morning a new arrival.*
> *A joy, a depression, a meanness,*
> *some momentary awareness comes*
> *as an unexpected visitor.*
> *Welcome and entertain them all!*
> *Even if they are a crowd of sorrows,*
> *who violently sweep your house*
> *empty of its furniture,*

still, treat each guest honorably.
He may be clearing you out
for some new delight.
The dark thought, the shame, the malice,
meet them at the door laughing and invite them in.
Be grateful for whatever comes
because each has been sent
as a guide from beyond.

What does it take to "welcome them all in"? Once I learn to do that, will I have peace? Will I no longer carry fear and anxiety with me into the unknown? If my faith is true and strong, will I be protected and gently cared for and spared the travails and disasters of life? If they do come is it because I wasn't "good enough" or faithful enough? This was my question to all I met as I began this quest. I am pleased to share that I have found the answer. Perhaps a better phrase would be that I have been blessed with an answer.

The answer, for me, is that life will happen no matter how strong or great my faith. Life will present challenges and disappointments no matter how many positive affirmations I create to try to avoid suffering. Pain is a part of our human existence, and no one gets to go through life without it. Sometimes it's in small things, like a festering splinter or a bad cold, and sometimes it's heart-wrenching and debilitating. We all know what those events can look like.

There's a popular phrase used in the media right now, and to paraphrase, it says, "Stuff happens." We may be able to welcome it all in, like Rumi suggests, but it's the challenge of a lifetime. What I have discovered is that after an experience—yes, after, not normally during—I will get to choose how I want to perceive the "stuff." Will I see it for the blessing it can be, the lessons I may have received? Or will it remain nothing but continued pain and suffering? I began to make peace with who I am and how I previously responded to the challenges of my life, and I realized that with my faith, from all these years of practicing my faith, I will have the free will to choose how I shape that experience, no matter how I labeled it at the moment of its conception. I am a strong, resourceful, loving person, and I fully recognize that things will happen that will knock me down. But I also believe that I have created the inner and outer resources to rise up again and to believe that I can "meet them at the door laughing and invite them in. Be grateful for whatever comes because each has been sent as a guide from beyond."

So in answer to Sarah Susanka's last question, for the following year I want to focus on the fact that I can choose to believe the year will be exciting because I know I get to choose my response to whatever happens to me. I choose "Awesome." In fact, I choose "Awesome" for the rest of my life.

7. God's GPS

Affirmation: *I am in awe of the guidance God sends me as I travel down a new path.*

What is needed in order to navigate through new territory? Lewis and Clark, Columbus and Magellan and Dr. Livingston are a few examples of pioneers who headed out into the world without any foreknowledge of what lay ahead and created trails for others to follow. There are now maps for most anywhere we want to go. There is even Google Earth, where we can examine almost every square foot of our planet without leaving our home.

When my daughter Ellen moved to London, I desperately wanted to see where she would be living, but flying over there was not in our plans. She sent me a video from Google Earth with her apartment circled in red. I could then move the cursor around on the page and see everything she could see from her front window. It was miraculous. Since then I have occasionally gone to the site to see the areas where I resided when I was younger. It was fascinating to see how the areas had changed and to share the photos of the neighborhood with my children or my friends.

It seems to me as if the whole world is mapped out and we aren't in need of pioneers any longer. Even the moon and Mars have "rovers" with cameras on them. Of course there is the rest of the Universe "where no man has ever gone before." I don't believe many of us will be faced with an adventure into outer space. In addition to outer space, however, there is also the Olympics. No one needed a map to get to the Winter Olympics in Sochi, Russia, and no one followed a geographical path that hadn't been carefully laid out, but these gifted, dedicated, and determined young people were definitely blazing new trails. The gold medal winner for the Men's Snowboarding Half-Pipe, Iouri Podladtchikov, not only performed an almost flawless run; he created and executed a new maneuver called the YOLO. The men and women skiers and skaters broke all-time speed records, and the Russian figure skating pairs gold medalists Tatiana Volosozhar and Maxim Trankov, the 2013 world champions, broke at least four world records with their performances. There were also many other records set. All the athletes needed guidance to reach the peak of their skill. They went higher and further along the path of their craft than anyone had gone before. Their coaches and families helped them lay out the map for their successes.

I've always loved a map. Maybe it's because it's a little like a puzzle, a maze which can help get you to your set destination. I've usually been the navigator when my husband and I traveled. My expertise wasn't always in evidence. For example, from my reading of the map, I once insisted we were on the right road to reach the main highway when it dead-ended in someone's driveway. At one time, I used to contact AAA for little map booklets that had a different section of the road on each page to lay out our path. I'm sure they don't have them anymore. My husband and I don't use maps any longer. First we graduated to MapQuest and had sheets of paper listing the twists and turns and the distances and the estimated arrival time. We even used MapQuest for one of our European trips. It was a lot easier than trying to read maps in a foreign language. Then we went to a Nuvi or a Garmin, and we had audible, turn-by-turn instructions. I must say in the beginning, it seemed the device would sometimes take me to my final destination by way of another continent. Then we went to the smartphone. The technology seems to have become much more accurate than at its initial inception, and I admit I now rely on it anywhere I travel. I've also become so used to having a computer map on my car dashboard that I feel lost when I'm in a car without one, even if I'm going around my neighborhood. At the time of this missive, however, I had had to chart a new path.

There wasn't a map or a GPS for this journey. When I wrote this my 91-year-old mother, Margaret Grolimund, had left the hospital after her first two surgeries ever, a hip replacement and a pacemaker, and was admitted to a rehab unit. I needed a map or an audio guide. I needed any direction and guidance available, and there was very little out there. I did do some research on the web to determine the best facility in the area and I did make the necessary phone calls to make sure that's where she was admitted, but after that I felt like I had just landed on an alien planet, not country, but a planet beyond our solar system. I have never been so intimately involved in the care of a seriously ill individual, and to be honest my mom had led a very independent lifestyle up until her fall. I wish someone wise and experienced had taken my hand and led me step by step down this road.

I wish I knew in the beginning of this journey what I came to know. I'd prayed for years for dignity for my mom and mother-in-law in their old age. Now, I was seeing what dignity could look like and did not look like.

After entering the rehab, Mom contracted C. diff (clostridium difficile colitis). One more thing I knew nothing about; another huge detour on the road. I reached out to God and to everyone I knew. I actually sent an email to several of my communities that was titled "Help!" Help came and kept coming. Help not just for my mom but for me, the main caregiver. Yes, I saw the blessings. Some of the best help was what I considered to be "God's GPS." It consisted of all those people in the know who took the time and effort to share with me what I needed to be doing and in what direction I needed to be going.

When Sandy, my hubby, and I traveled to Ireland, we found the most joyful part of the trip was getting lost, because we would stop and ask an always delightful, friendly Irish man or woman for directions. We stopped once on a back road and were invited in for tea! That was my experience with my mom and her illness; the people who reached out to me explaining the path best chosen brought clarity and joy to a very frightening and strange road. I decided there is very seldom an easy way through chronic illness or the dying process, but like all our adversities there are blessings to be found. Usually they come in the form of loving, caring people who take our hands and our hearts and lead us along the path of life. I like to think of them as God's GPS, audibly directing us down the road to our final destination, Peace.

8. A Secret Ingredient

Affirmation: *Even when I am doing little things of service, I include a large amount of love.*

What's your favorite food? Everyone has a favorite. It's a great question to start a conversation or to open a group discussion because it seems as if most people have an immediate answer. My favorite food has always been my mother's chocolate chip cookies. Her cookies were probably the reason I could never lose those extra five pounds I've always wanted to lose. She told me it was simply the recipe on the back of the Toll House Chocolate Chip package, but I didn't believe her. I think there was a secret ingredient, perhaps one of which she was not even aware. It was a mystery! I'm not the only one who loved her chocolate chip cookies. They were a favorite for the whole family, especially my son Joey. For years she baked him a special batch. "Those are only for Joey." I think he was one of her favorite grandsons. I've also had other people tell me she baked special batches of cookies for them. "She told me these were only for me."

I have many friends who like to bake. It's a gift to be a baker. It runs in our family. My mother passed on her love and skill to both my daughters, Melissa and Ellen, my sister's daughter Samantha, and my brother's daughter Stacy. The food doesn't just taste good; it looks yummy. I was stunned when during one of my visits to Ellen, she asked me if I'd like to see her journal. I couldn't even imagine where this offer was leading. Was she going to confess some deep, dark secret or, worse yet, have one of those mother-daughter "come to Jesus" conversations? Then she pulled out her baking journal. It was beautiful. She had all the recipes she'd been trying, with the adjustments recorded to make them more to her liking, and photos of the cookies and cakes. I was honored to have her share her passion with me.

Most bakers want to share their treats with their friends, family, and whoever would enjoy them. I watched my mom and other bakers go about giving away their cookies to whomever they wanted to grace.

It didn't need to be a special occasion. It might just be because someone needed a pick-me-up or perhaps it was a way to say, "Thank you." My mom would give her yummy cookies to the hairdresser, the auto mechanic, the nurse and doctors she frequented, to an ailing friend or perhaps to her friend's caregiver. They were always warmly and graciously received. Many times our Christmas presents to her were fancy "cookie" boxes with her initials on them or several cookie tins with varying designs. She even began saving some of the small plastic containers from the grocery so she could package up just two or three cookies and present them. I envy people who like to bake. I, too, would like to be seen as a warm, generous person who says "thank you" with a tangible, yummy treat, but I don't like to bake, especially cookies. So, I wondered what I could share in a similar manner.

I decided there is no substitute. There is nothing as heartwarming as a homemade treat. Let's face it, even if you're not eating sugar or can't eat sugar, the gift still warms your heart. You know someone really cares and they've taken the time and energy necessary to let you know. Perhaps sharing food in any way brings those same warm feelings. I've been to many events where people showed up with food as a form of love and support. My experience of living in the Midwest and now here in the South affirms that belief. If someone has a tragedy or is going through a difficult time, people bring meals. During my many months of cancer treatment, we were supported with some of the best meals I've ever eaten. On the flip side, I've dropped off meals whenever the opportunity presented itself. I usually make dinner and include some sort of chocolate candy. I don't bake. I do, however, make every effort to be affable and caring on a daily basis.

As I go through my day, I readily share a smile. I have found it uplifts not only my spirits but usually the recipient's too. I'm an avid hugger. I learned that skill from my husband, Sandy, and my mother-in-law, Yolanda. I know not everyone wants to be hugged. If I'm not sure I open my arms and hesitate. It's usually fairly obvious if it's not welcomed. That doesn't happen very often. I love to send snail-mail birthday cards with a blessing over them and a few loving words inside. I know these small gestures do not hold a candle to a good chocolate chip cookie, but it's my way of letting people know they are loved; they are an important part of my life. I value them and our relationship.

When my mom passed away, we included in her obituary the fact that she was famous for her chocolate chip cookies. When I spoke to the presider of her Requiem Mass, Father Doug Reed, I shared her notoriety, and he wanted to know her recipe. I told him what she said, that it was simply the recipe on the back of the Toll House Chocolate Chip package. But I know she was not sharing the secret ingredient. She didn't know what it was. It was magical! Her secret ingredient was her love. She made those cookies, cakes, and pies with a heart filled with love. We all show love in different ways. This was my mom's way, and she did it marvelously. Love is the secret ingredient in every special gift we share with another. It's that one thing that tells someone, "These are only for you. I love you."

9. Believing in Angels

Affirmation: *I choose to believe in angels.*

Do you ever think about angels? Not the Los Angeles baseball team, but the ones who appear in mythology and theology. They are a part of all the major religions. Do you believe in angels? Do you think they all have wings? Are they male and female or gender neutral? Do they ever appear in their true form or do they take on human characteristics? Do you think we really have guardian angels? What if you did believe, truly believe, that there was a powerful spiritual presence hovering over you, advising you, guiding you? How would that feel? Would it make you feel calmer? Would you become more conscious of your choices?

There have been many movies made about angels. My favorite is very old. It's the black-and-white version of *The Bishop's Wife* with Cary Grant, David Niven, and Loretta Young. There was the TV series that ran from 1994–2003 called *Touched by an Angel,* and of course, Hallmark loves stories that have an angel theme. I've also read several book about angels. There are stories about people who see angels, talk to angels, and receive guidance from angels. One of the books I read many years ago offered a journaling process to help you "hear" the wisdom of the angels involved in your life. And, of course, there is the ultimate angel book—the Bible.

The whole salvation story begins with the angel Gabriel's announcement to Mary that she is to be the mother of the Messiah. The angels go on to announce the birth of our Savior to the shepherds and then continue to guide and protect the Holy Family throughout the beginning of the New Testament. Was that it? Did they stop visiting after that?

For many years one of my affirmations has been *"I have a very active guardian angel."* I don't know when I began to truly believe that she (yes, she) was actively looking after me, but looking back on my life, I completely believe that someone very powerful was helping me make decisions that were to my benefit rather than my detriment. There has always been a greater force in my life, planting thoughts and ideas that led me along a path resulting in the life I now relish, a force that was not recognizable, not tangible. I look back and I am in awe of how I've been guided. Let's face it, we all have those moments when if we went left instead of right, we know without any doubt that our lives would have been much harder, maybe even shorter. I simply look back and feel blessed. I know it has been my guardian angel, Saranna.

I'd been talking to Saranna for many years when my dear deceased friend and massage therapist, Valerie Kelly, one day announced that there was an angel in the room with us. She took a deep breath and seemed quite startled. I was not surprised. Then she asked me if I wanted to know her name. I had named my angel many years before. Someone told me it was a good idea. I had named her Anna. It seemed like a nice angel name. Valerie stopped and listened for a moment and then said, "Her name is Saranna." And so she is.

I call on her guidance quite often. I invite her to lead or pave the way. Sometimes I request that she speak with her friends, my loved one's angels, and ask them to smooth or direct the way. I know if you are a realist and don't believe in the spiritual world, you probably have stopped reading by now. If you're a therapist without any faith in a power greater than us, you have diagnosed me as someone with a problem or at the very least an overactive imagination. I haven't heard the angels and sadly I haven't seen them in their natural state, but I know they are here. I simply know it.

My husband, Sandy, will not pass a homeless person without giving him or her money. He always tells me that they could be an angel in disguise. The weekend of April 25, 2015 was the twenty-first *Angels Among Us Walk* for the Preston Robert Tisch Brain Tumor Center at Duke. They open the walk with the song "Angels Among Us," and the survivors lead the way for several thousand walkers who are there to raise awareness and money for brain tumor research. That year they raised over $2,094,000. Two of the first patients treated with the new polio virus technique led the way. They are free of glioblastomas, an unheard of accomplishment until the last couple of years. I didn't "see" any angels that Saturday, but I am sure there were many of them present.

In May my friend and massage therapist Blaire Schultz invited me to be part of a chain begun in 2000. She explained that I would be inviting the Archangels into my home for five days and when they left I would invite three other friends to host them. Why not? I followed the directions and set up the little welcome station, which had a candle, a white flower, three slips of paper with a personal request, a family request, a community request, and an apple to absorb the blessings of their presence. They arrived at 10:30 p.m. on the date I was told, and as far as I was concerned, they were using my home as their base for the next five days. Were there any unusual happenings? Were there any miracles? Did I see or notice anything unusual? No, no, and no, but I felt different. I had a sense of peace and comfort that was beyond my normal. Just the thought that they were blessing my home and family gave me comfort. They are "gone" now, but I've decided since I've opened my home to them, I can now consider them to be close friends, and when I have a pressing need, they will return.

I looked up the mythology around the Archangels. It seems there are somewhere between three and seven. I don't know how many were here during their visit. I know Michael, Rafael, and Gabriel were here for sure. I attend St. Michael the Archangel Church. I live off Rafael Drive, and have several people in my life named Gabriel. It's all a mystery, isn't it? I am comfortable with mystery at this time in my life. I don't have to understand everything that I believe. That's what faith is all about, believing the unbelievable. *I choose to believe in angels.* I choose to believe there is a higher, compassionate, wise power that wants to lead us to a better, more fulfilling life, and that belief brings me peace and comfort and hope.

10. Legion of Angels

Affirmation: *I am empowered and feel nurtured when I stop and recognize the presence of my angels and guides.*

When I first listened to Belleruth Naparstek's CD, *A Meditation to Help You with Chemotherapy,* I was greatly comforted by her description of spiritual beings who came to assist me with my healing, "some of which look familiar." As I listened I clearly envisioned the presence of several ethereal beings, and yes, one looked very familiar. He was my father, Francis Grolimund, long deceased but whose memory and presence always seem to be lingering about me. I've played that recording dozens of times. I love to end a yoga session with it. It's full of hope and tools to encourage healing.

I'd been dealing with a chronic ache over a period of one and a half years and found myself feeling weak and discouraged. I'd done all within my power to help my body heal, much of which revolved around alternative healing. I did go the western medicine route also, but that, too, did not present an answer.

When I journal I'm usually writing a stream of consciousness. I do always try to focus on three joys from the day before and list one for the day to come, but otherwise it's just my form of rambling and dumping. It's a gift I give myself. I love the practice. One day, however, I remembered my friend's approach to her morning ritual. Joan Junginger often talks about her "coffee with Jesus." Periodically I'd tried writing to God or the angels. It never seemed to resolve anything, but I was becoming quite desperate and decided this one morning to give it another try. I would write that letter to Jesus and see if anything new appeared.

When Joan Junginger, cofounder of The Heart's Journey, leads retreats, one of which she did for a large group of women at St. Michael the Archangel and which I had attended, she normally encourages the participants to write such a letter and then to write a letter to themselves from Jesus. I heard some remarkable stories from a few of the women who had been doing this exercise for several years. I'm sure that's why the journaling on this one morning was taking on a new twist.

As I wrote out my concerns to the Lord, I found a name appearing that I hadn't thought about in a very long time. This woman, Suzanne Egan, is a massage therapist and a health and wellness coach. She's lived and worked in my area for many years and is knowledgeable about the different physicians and practices. I had struggled with a hip issue for many years when I first showed up at her practice, and with her guidance I was led to Sangini Rane of Apex PT, who specializes in Postural Restoration Therapy and who guided me to a pain-free hip.

After my journaling was done, I immediately contacted Suzanne. Luckily she was still at the same number. She responded right away and had several suggestions for my latest challenge that I had not fully investigated. Even better was the fact that she had a couple of clients who had dealt successfully with the same issue. She contacted them and got their referrals and then made a few more recommendations of her own. I know you've had this experience too. I was being given the gift of hope.

Then, too, as I wrote I began to value all the years and hours I had put into my prayer life. I don't always take credit for the fact that I've been practicing my faith for my whole life, and I've been especially fervent for the last forty-plus years. Each morning I invite all my angels and especially my guardian angel, Saranna, and my guides to join me. It's the prayer I say when I wake and as I begin my journaling. It's on the last page of my first book, *Creating Positive Affirmations, Living an Intentional Life,* and at the end of this book.

> *Lord, be united with me this day and always. I invite You and all those who nurture and guide me, seen and unseen, to aid me in bringing glory and honor and praise to this gift of life You have so generously given me.*

This particular morning I found myself picturing those spiritual beings manifesting themselves around me, but it felt different. For the first time I felt the presence of a legion of beings, not just the few I'd always called upon. I felt like a curtain had been raised. I hadn't been able to see everyone who answered my call until that day. I had been limiting God's response. I was shocked to realize my small-mindedness.

I've always known we get to choose whether to go to God in prayer with a thimble, a bucket, or a pipeline, but I hadn't let the knowledge go from my head into my heart. And this day, for the first time, it weaved its way right down into the center of my being. I created a new affirmation to cement the concept and began saying it and writing it every day since then. *I believe I am surrounded and supported by Christ and His legions of angels and spiritual guides. I am empowered and feel nurtured when I stop and recognize their presence.* I've even had visions of those animated armies you see in some of the sci-fi films. The ones where the beings cover the entire landscape and keep coming over the hills and ridges. I know it sounds extreme, maybe a little (?) crazy, but just like all my affirmations, it brings me a sense of calm and even power which I had misplaced while dealing with this issue.

I followed Suzanne's recommendations and I said my affirmation daily to tap into the Divine army available to me and my loved ones. I couldn't tell you at the time if I was cured, but something very deep within me shifted and I no longer carried around that initial sense of weakness and powerlessness. I'd been here before with other physical challenges, especially with my hip and many years ago with breast cancer, and I must say this is a good place. My heart and my head are finally united, and I'm in a place of hope and positive expectation.

I share this with you in case you, too, have been going to God with just a small container, not attaching the pipeline that is right there in front of you. Perhaps you, too, will begin to envision a legion of spiritual beings surrounding you and protecting you and giving you the support for whatever you're dealing with—so that you, too, will experience hope and peace and feel strong and powerful.

"May the power of angels come to greet you; may they lead you to paradise," both here and in the hereafter.

11. Blessing Adversity

Affirmation: *What doesn't kill me makes me stronger, and being stronger makes life easier and richer.*

"What doesn't kill you makes you stronger, stronger." So goes the saying and the once-popular song by Kelly Clarkson. I wondered, would I want to be tested to the point of dying to become stronger? I have been tested by breast cancer. I wouldn't have chosen it, but it made me stronger. It seems like a given that most people believe becoming stronger is a good thing.

I have consistently worked at being physically strong. I fully recognize the advantages of having a strong body. Besides practicing yoga at least twice a week, I have always had a program involving weight training. Having physical strength makes my daily activities easier. I also work at having mental and spiritual fortitude. It makes my whole existence easier.

Sherri Shepherd's book is *Plan D: How to Lose Weight and Beat Diabetes*. At this time she was one of the talk show hostesses on *The View*. She was funny, and she had always been a large lady—actually the word is *obese*. She was interviewed by Doctor Oz and shared the diabetic history of her family. She said they called it "the sugar," and no one took any steps to deal with it, regardless of how much the disease had progressed. She, too, was guilty of the same behavior. Denial is the term for the way some people deal with situations they don't want to face. She was in denial until someone asked her in so many words if she was ready to die one amputation at a time. She changed her life. She took charge. She changed her diet and began exercising. She changed a life-threatening situation into a life-enhancing practice. She shared some of her new healthy eating techniques and said she was now working out at a gym and had turned her home into a gym, not a fancy room with all the bells and whistles. The stairs were her Stairmaster. The kitchen sink was her ballet barre, and she never rested her bottom on the toilet. That was her opportunity to do squats! Diabetes changed her life, for the better.

One conversation I had with a woman I once met revolved around her brother's recovery from drug abuse. He, too, had a devastating disease. He, too, had taken steps to become healthy. When speaking about his life, she shared that he had become a wonderful father. He was raising his son by himself. The mother was also an addict and had given up her son. He had shared with his sister that the challenge of being a single parent was his greatest blessing. His life was as good as it was because his son needed him and helped him rise to the challenge of creating a healthy, loving life.

It's an old saying, but we can choose to make lemons into lemonade. Life is full of adversity, all different levels. We all face diseases of the mind, body, and spirit at some time or another. Where do we find the resources to lift ourselves from the darkness back into the light? For many it's their faith, but not everyone has that gift. It is a gift to believe in a loving, benevolent God or at least to believe that our pain is serving some higher purpose. We all have pain. Others must find another way to rise above their adversity. For most, help comes in the form of others: family, friends, and community.

One week in 2013, the media was full of news about Angelina Jolie and her choice to have a prophylactic double mastectomy. It's not an unusual story. It's a decision thousands of women have faced, and many of whom have chosen the same path. Angelina's mother was diagnosed with ovarian cancer in her forties. She died at fifty-five. Angelina decided to undergo the gene test to see if it was indeed a hereditary condition, and it came back positive. She had an 87 percent chance of dying of breast cancer. She chose not to wait for fate to decide her future. She chose to take radical steps to ensure that she would not have the words "breast cancer" on her death certificate. Her popularity, perhaps we could even say notoriety, propelled her decision to the front of the news. I personally commend her for making her decision public. It opened the avenue for important discussions. It's similar to when Betty Ford stepped forward as First Lady and shared she was undergoing treatment for breast cancer. We sometimes need celebrities to shed light on issues that might otherwise go unexamined.

How can one see a prophylactic double mastectomy as a blessing? How easy it would be to perceive oneself as a victim. How easy it would be to wallow in self-pity. Brad Pitt, Angelina's fiancé at the time, told the media they didn't view her surgery as a loss. They viewed it as a gain; they had gained years of life.

When we are in the middle of some challenge, it's almost impossible to see it as beneficial. I believe we need to move away and outside of it before we can begin to see ways it may and can bless our lives. It's all about the whole package; all of life's lessons are valuable. We are all going to be faced with adversity. Most of us will come through it; there's no going around it. How we perceive our experience will be determined by how we view our lives. Do we wake each morning and see the blessings the day may bestow upon us or do we rise in fear and dread? What are we focusing on? How do you view the glass, half empty or half full? I'm not talking about not recognizing your sadness and fear. We must acknowledge all our emotions, but once we've done that and walked through the "valley of death," do we want to continue to suffer? Maybe some do, but I would prefer to let the experience teach me whatever lesson I needed to know and then take that knowledge and use it to make me "stronger! stronger! stand a little taller!" as Kelly sings, and to enjoy a tall, cool glass of that lemonade.

12. Expanding My Gaze

Affirmation: *I choose peace and love.*

Have you heard of Yogaville? It is a yoga ashram located on 750 acres in Virginia. It was founded by Swami Satchidananda. The shrine, called the LOTUS (Light of Truth Universal Shrine), was opened in 1986. I was looking for something to do with my granddaughter Isabelle (age seventeen at the time) for my birthday because my husband, Sandy, had told me he would be traveling. Isabelle and I had been practicing yoga together for a while before this, and I thought it would be a great adventure for us to share. It turned out to be only a three-hour drive from our home. I signed us up for a course called "Healthy Relationships in Yoga & The Path of Heart."

God bless my granddaughter! What a light she is and what a good sport! The diet was strictly vegan, and we were quite challenged to find something to eat other than kale and tofu. Also, she was the youngest by about ten years. Her youthful spirit and presence alone brought joy and smiles to everyone we encountered. We laughed, we ate weird food, we met new, interesting people, and most importantly we created some wonderful memories.

One of the first things we were told when we arrived was not to miss seeing the shrine. We were in the middle of nowhere, and I envisioned a small concrete or wooden structure with maybe a Hindu deity in the middle. The next morning we headed out to walk about a mile through the woods to take photos and see what there was to see. We reached a road and followed it up a hill and then from out of the valley below rose a giant pink and blue lotus-shaped building. It was, I guessed, as large as the White House in DC, but it wasn't white. We were stunned. It was one of a huge complex consisting of three buildings that started at the top of the mountain and ended down in the valley. What would we find inside?

On Tuesday, February 2, 2015, Kate Cook was the yoga teacher at Fire Fly Hot Yoga in Cary, NC. She led a ninety-minute Intensive Slow

Flow class. She's one of the best yoginis with whom I have ever studied. She is so precise in her language and she always brings a lesson with her to deepen our practice. One week she instructed us to gaze on the ball of energy we created when we cupped our hands and placed them in front of us. As we breathed in, our hands moved together; as we breathed out, they expanded. Then, as we were doing our balance poses, she encouraged us to "change our gaze."

Normally when one is balancing, the instruction is to focus on one point. In yoga it's called a "drishti." Kate reminded us that our mat practice is a metaphor for our life practice. We have the opportunity to take what we learn on our mats with us out into the world. As far as I'm concerned, developing balance is one of the most important qualities we can cultivate for ourselves. I do like to remind myself, however, that as one yoga teacher said, "There is no balance, there is only balancing." We are either coming into balance or falling out. I know this is true for me.

As I stood there on one leg with my fingers wrapped around my big toe and lifted my leg straight out to one side, my drishti was on some unmovable object in front of me. I was trying to stay upright and trying to remember to breathe. Kate then suggested we "change our gaze" and look in one direction and then the other. I fell over and I tried again and I fell over again. I lost my balance. Without a focus I couldn't stay steady; with a focus I couldn't see the rest of the space. Which is better? I decided neither. Sometimes one is needed and other times, a greater perspective is essential.

It's good to be focused. It helps me accomplish the tasks I set before myself, but when it limits my perspective on life, it shrinks my world into a smaller box and I need to get smaller to fit into it. I don't want to be small. At five feet tall, I'm small enough. I want to take a big giant breath and expand my world to include all sorts of people, places, and ideas. Then I have to decide what to allow to stay with me and what I want to let go. What is "of God" and what is not? What will enhance my life and what will diminish it? It's a meditation, don't you think? We are faced with this choice day in and day out. Sometimes it's about food. Sometimes it's about activities. It can be about people, and most certainly it's about our ideas, our beliefs, and our concepts.

The shrine in Yogaville is dedicated to all religions in the world, those that are well known and those that are yet to come. There are twelve altars in the lower level with reminders of Judaism, Christianity, Hinduism, the Moslem faith, and eight others. It is respectful and well presented. It is a home for all, even the atheist. My initial reaction was small-minded, but I prefer to be an inclusive person, and Kate's yoga class helped me respond in a more open, accepting, nonjudgmental mode.

I have read Pope Francis' encyclical, "The Joy of the Gospel." He, too, talks about accepting all faiths, not judging, even accepting the nonbelievers. Peace. I believe this is Peace. I know we are instructed to "spread the good news." We are actually commanded to do so. The best way I know to do that is to try to always be a kind and compassionate person. But when someone tells you they are right and you are "so very wrong," what is your reaction? It's not normally a peaceful one, is it? The course Isabelle and I took was led by two of the founders of Yogaville, Jeevakan and Priya Abbate. They were kind, gentle, compassionate people. I could see why so many were attracted to this place. It radiated peace and acceptance. One of the lessons was: "We can be right or we can have peace." I've also heard it phrased, "We can be right or we can love." This is the difference between having a focus and seeing the broader picture.

Here I sit with a focus on Christ, but for me, God is everywhere. God is everything. I am not here to limit God's unfathomable power. Yogaville was a good place for me to share an adventure with Isabelle. It was a great birthday weekend. I was outside of my comfort zone. I had to broaden my horizons and see God in all things, even within a giant pink and blue concrete flower rising out of the Virginia valley.

13. Throwing Away the Trash

Affirmation: *I freely forgive myself and others.*

The topic of the NPR story was about the abolition of the death penalty. What type of response do you have to the phrase "death penalty"? You must have given it some thought. The Old Testament promotes "an eye for an eye, a tooth for a tooth, a hand for a hand, a foot for a foot" (Exodus 21:24). Then, Jesus came along and promoted a whole new concept—forgiveness. Even at the end when He had been unjustly toured and crucified, He prayed for His executioners, for all of us. "Father, forgive them for they know not what they do" (Luke 23:24).

I think of this quote often. Someone once commented to me that He did not say, "Father, I forgive them for they know not what they do" or even "Father, I forgive them even if they know what they are doing." I'm sure there are many biblical scholars who have dissected these last words of Christ and are much more qualified to fully explain all the implications of His petition; I am not one of them. I am simply trying to absorb the lesson that even after Our Lord was put to death because some people did not approve of Him healing the sick, raising the dead, and protecting and promoting the care of those who most needed love and care, He refused to hold onto the burning coal of hatred. In His final moments He was teaching us His greatest lesson.

As I drove along that day, the story being discussed on the radio was about the death penalty in China and the tradition that allows a family member of the victim to actively participate in the execution of the offender by removing the support from under the person who is to be hung. The narrator told of a young man who had been stabbed to death by another young man, and the mother of the victim had chosen to perform the execution. She approached the condemned, reached up, and slapped him and then reached out and helped him down from his perch. She then went over and took the hand of the mother of the condemned man. The story resonated throughout

China, and now it was being shared with the rest of the world. Because of her action, the Chinese authorities were reconsidering their tradition. Because of her act of forgiveness, some of the world's conscience was being awakened.

Why do most of us find it so difficult to forgive, me included? I am not normally angry. I'll get hurt before I respond with anger. Perhaps that's just another form of anger. Sometimes, however, I'm angry at institutions, authorities, or systems. Sometime I'm angry at individuals. I can be angry at strangers, friends, and worst of all, people I love. Some small injurious word or behavior and I can feel the resentment building. Most of the time just when I think I'm "over" something that has happened, I don't even realize I haven't let go of the perceived injury or intentional slight or harm. But then some reminder comes along, and I'm back with my sad response. I can recall events from decades ago that still cause my body to tighten up, but most times I don't even recognize the emotion. Sometimes when the anger arrives, I am puzzled by the feeling because it is so rare for me to respond in an angry manner.

The question that sometimes comes to my mind is "What do I know to be true? What do I believe absolutely with all of my mind and my heart?"

"The only important thing in life is to love and to forgive." This is a quote from a wise older woman who was from my small Christian community. I believe with all my mind, body, and soul that the above statement is absolutely true. Richard Rohr, one of my favorite spiritual teachers, explains the Beatitudes in this way: "Jesus seems to be saying our inner attitudes and states are the real sources of our problems. How we live in our hearts is our real truth." When I can carry only love in my heart and my body and when I can release myself from any resentment, my life is rich and rewarding and peaceful. My life is then filled with hope and joy, and I am able to take those emotions, those qualities with me out into the world.

One of my morning meditations took me into a subway station. What am I doing here? I pondered. On the station were six briefcases evenly spaced along the edge. The train came and five people picked up a case and boarded. I went over to the sixth case and looked down. It had my name on it and so I opened it. It was filled with trash. It was filled with the resentments of yesterday, perhaps of my whole life. I carried it up out of the subway, found a trash can, and threw it away. Perhaps like most of the garbage in my life, I need to gather those resentments up periodically and toss them out. Perhaps with practice, I can throw away all those resentments and other junk that interfere with the love and joy with which I want my life to be surrounded.

The Chinese woman in the story was changing the world because of her ability to forgive. I believe we are called upon to do the same and that with the softening of our hearts, we, too, will change the world.

Epilogue

Dear Friend,

Thank you for sharing this journey with me. I hope these affirmations and stories have both nurtured and empowered you. I hope they have caused you to reflect on your life and how you want to shape it. I begin each of my journal entries with the following prayer. As with this whole book, I share it here with you in case it will serve you, but it's even more powerful, just like the affirmations, if you create a prayer of your own.

Loving Jesus,

I invite You to share this peaceful, nurturing, insightful time with me. Time to just be, centering time, creative time. Time to love and to count my blessings. Time to see more clearly my gifts and the gifts held and bestowed by others. Time to shine light on my shadows and to ask for and receive forgiveness. Time for joy and for sadness, my lifetime here on these pages.

Lord, be united with me this day and always. I invite You and all those who nurture and guide me, seen and unseen, to aid me in bringing glory and honor and praise to this gift of life You have so generously given me.

You know my soul. You know all that is within. Fill me with pure love of You.

Loving Lord Jesus, Blessed Mother, all my angels and guides be with me all my days in every moment. I invite you to join me and to share in the glory of this life. Amen

Acknowledgments

I am married to a remarkable man as you may have gathered from these stories. Sandy and I have created a wonderful, love-filled life and family. It's the greatest gift God has bestowed upon me, allowing me to share this life with this amazing man and with my children: Melissa, Joey, and Ellen; their spouses Larry, Belen, and Adam; my grandchildren Joe, Sam, Isabelle, Owen, and Lorelei; and my other family members and dear, dear friends.

Thank you also to:

Yun Soo-Hoo for providing her award-winning painting, "Starry Sky" for the cover.

Pam Burnette, who once again took the time to edit this manuscript and affirmed every single entry. The gift of her friendship and encouragement is priceless to me.

Ellan Cates-Smith for her ongoing encouragement and for her generous forward.

My amazing study group, the Seekers: Joanne Dawe, Jean Scholz, Joanne Dreyer, Travis Tracy, Eileen Sakey, Susan Auman, Luanne Roth and Jean Young. Our journey together has brought me insight, joy, and excitement and has gifted me with an ongoing attitude of adventure about the future.

I also want to thank all those dear friends who read a draft of *Choosing Your Words, Crafting Your Life* and gave me their upbeat, kind, and constructive feedback.